S0-BAO-455

# SPIN!

## Grammar, Vocabulary, and Writing

B

## Genevieve J. Kocienda

## Writer: Ellen Balla

### LONGMAN ON THE WEB

Longman.com offers online resources for teachers and students. Access our Companion Websites, our online catalog, and our local offices around the world.

Longman English Success offers online courses to give learners flexible study options. Courses cover General English, Business English, and Exam Preparation.

Visit us at longman.com and englishsuccess.com.

Longman

**Spin! B Teacher's Guide**

Pearson Education, 10 Bank Street, White Plains, NY 10606

Vice president, director of instructional design: Allen Ascher
Executive editor: Anne Stribling
Senior development editor: Virginia Bernard
Vice president, director of design and production: Rhea Banker
Executive managing editor: Linda Moser
Production manager: Liza Pleva
Production editors: Sylvia Dare, Sasha Kintzler
Art director: Patricia Wosczyk
Director of manufacturing: Patrice Fraccio
Senior manufacturing buyer: Edith Pullman
Cover design: Elizabeth Carlson
Cover art: Mary Jane Begin
Cover photo: © Getty Images
Text design: Patricia Wosczyk
Text composition: TSI Graphics
Text art: Teresa Anderko

ISBN: 0-13-041986-9

2 3 4 5 6 7 8 9 10—BAH—07 06 05 04 03

# Contents

# Introduction

**Spin!** is a six-level course that makes learning grammar fun and engaging for students. Each level of **Spin!** contains the following components:

- Student Book
- Teacher's Guide
- Audio Program
- Reproducible Picture Cards

## The Student Book

The Student Book contains ten units and five review units. Each unit features an interesting and practical theme within an appropriate vocabulary and grammar context. After the vocabulary is introduced on the first page of the unit, it is used in a series of exercises which explain and practice the grammar point. Each unit also includes a chant and/or a game that allows students to practice the featured vocabulary and grammar in a fun and stimulating way. Review units, which appear after every two units, give students the opportunity to consolidate what they have learned through listening and pronunciation practice. At the back of each Student Book is a picture dictionary to help students develop research and dictionary skills.

## The Teacher's Guide

The Teacher's Guide features lesson plans and reduced Student Book pages. The reduced Student Book pages incorporate the answers for each exercise. Each lesson plan consists of a warm-up, an explanation of how to use each page of the Student Book, and games and activities to extend the lesson and reinforce the material learned. The beginning of each lesson includes a guide to grammar, the lesson vocabulary, materials needed, and helpful words and phrases that the teacher can use in the classroom to explain the lesson's activities. The review unit lesson plans also include the recording script of the Audio Program.

Physical movement to develop language skills in activities is adapted in **Spin!** from Total Physical Response (TPR), as developed by James J. Asher. This technique is ideal for students at the early stages of learning, when their capabilities for verbal response are as yet undeveloped. TPR provides both intense listening practice and repeated exposure to basic vocabulary items.

## The Audio Program

The Audio Program consists of a recording on cassette or CD. The Audio Program models the vocabulary words, the new grammar patterns, and the chants. Material featured in the Audio Program is indicated in the Student Book by the icon: 🎧.

## The Picture Cards

Reproducible Picture Cards of vocabulary words appear at the back of the Teacher's Guide. Sets of Picture Cards can be made for the students as well as the teacher. The Picture Cards are utilized in the lesson activities and can also be used in a variety of ways to enhance classroom learning.

# Acknowledgments

The publishers wish to thank the principals, coordinators, teachers, and students of the following schools and institutes. **Mexico City, Mexico:** Centro Educativo Exea, Colegio Martín Luis Guzman, Instituto Ateniense, Centro Escolar Walter Buchana, Colegio Motolinía, Colegio Fernando de Magallanes. **San Luis Potosí, Mexico:** Colegio Teresa Martín, Colegio Guadalupe Victoria, Instituto Kennedy, Colegio Tepeyac, Instituto Hispano Inglés, Colegio Juan de Dios Peza, Instituto Educación Siglo XXI, Instituto Asunción, Instituto Cultural Manuel José Othón, Colegio Miguel de Cervantes. **Caracas, Venezuela:** Colegio Americano, Colegio Claret, Colegio Canigua, Instituto Escuela, Colegio Santiago de León, Colegio Insight, Colegio Los Campitos. **Panama City, Panama:** Instituto Episcopal San Cristobal, Instituto Justo Arosemena, Colegio San Agustin, Colegio Nuestra Señora de Lourdes, Instituto Panamericano. **Guatemala City, Guatemala:** Verbo Christian School, Continental Americano, Lehnsen Roosevelt Bilingual School, Liceo Chapero, Sagrado Corazón, Centro Escobar El Roble, Liceo Bilingüe Las Naciones, Verbo El Valle.

# Time Guidelines

*Use introduction pages before Unit 1 as appropriate.*

| R = Review<br>P = Present | Week 1 | Week 2 | Week 3 | Week 4 |
|---|---|---|---|---|
| **Unit 1** | Vocabulary<br>**P:** *I'm/you're/<br>he's/she's* | **R:** *I'm/you're/he's/<br>she's, present<br>progressive*<br>**P:** *They're/we're/you're* | **R:** *contractions*<br>**P:** Irregular plurals | **R:** *as needed*<br>**P:** Chant; Game |
| **Unit 2** | Vocabulary<br>**P:** *behind, next to,<br>above* | **R:** *behind, next to,<br>above*<br>**P:** *There is/there are* | **R:** *There is/there are*<br>**P:** *How many?*<br>Chant; Game | **R:** *Units 1 and 2* |
| **Unit 3** | Vocabulary<br>**P:** *My/your* | **R:** *my/your*<br>**P:** Possessive *-s* | **R:** *possessives*<br>**P:** *Is there/are there?* | **R:** *as needed*<br>**P:** Chant; Game |
| **Unit 4** | Vocabulary<br>**P:** *On, between* | **R:** *on, between*<br>**P:** Adjectives | **R:** *adjectives*<br>**P:** Proper nouns<br>Chant; Game | **R:** *Units 3 and 4* |
| **Unit 5** | Vocabulary<br>**P:** *What (does<br>he/she do)?* | **R:** *What (does he/<br>she do)?*<br>**P:** *Who (is he/she)?* | **R:** *What?/Who?*<br>**P:** *Where (does a<br>doctor work)* | **R:** *as needed*<br>**P:** Chant; Game |
| **Unit 6** | Vocabulary<br>**P:** Simple present,<br>first person *(I)* | **R:** *simple present<br>with (I)*<br>**P:** Simple present,<br>third person *(he/she)* | **R:** *simple present<br>with I/he/she*<br>**P:** *When (do you/<br>does he/does<br>she . . . )?*<br>Chant; Game | **R:** *Units 5 and 6* |
| **Unit 7** | Vocabulary<br>**P:** Plural nouns *(-s<br>and -es endings)* | **R:** *plural nouns*<br>**P:** Noncount nouns | **R:** *noncount nouns*<br>**P:** *Some (oranges/<br>chicken)* | **R:** *as needed*<br>**P:** Chant; Game |
| **Unit 8** | Vocabulary<br>**P:** Punctuation *(!)* | **R:** *punctuation*<br>**P:** *Have/has* in<br>statements and<br>questions | **R:** *have/has*<br>**P:** *Its/their*<br>Chant; Game | **R:** *Units 7 and 8* |
| **Unit 9** | Vocabulary<br>**P:** *Always/never* | **R:** *always/never*<br>**P:** *Sometimes* | **R:** *always/never/<br>sometimes*<br>**P:** *When (is your<br>birthday)?* | **R:** *as needed*<br>**P:** Chant; Game |
| **Unit 10** | Vocabulary<br>**P:** *How (do you go<br>to school)?* | **R:** *How?*<br>**P:** *How (does he/<br>she go to school)?* | **R:** *How?*<br>**P:** *How (are you<br>feeling)?*<br>Chant; Game | **R:** *Units 9 and 10* |

# Numbers and Shapes

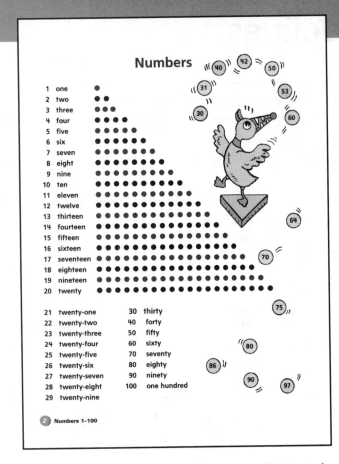

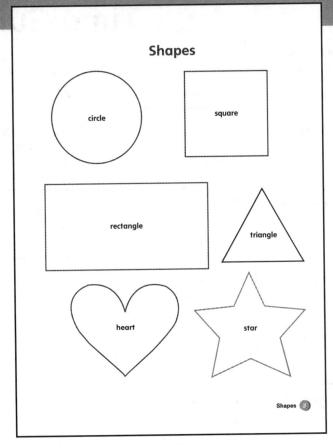

**Vocabulary:** numbers 1–100, circle, heart, rectangle, star, square, triangle

### Lesson Objectives
✓ to say and identify the numbers 1–100

### Classroom English
• Find. Say. Color. Listen. Write. Show me. Point to. What number is it? It is (twenty-one).

### Language Patterns
• It is a (triangle).
• It is (one hundred).

### Materials
cut out shapes

## WARMING UP
### Numbers

Write the numbers 1–100 on the board. Say each number, point to it, and invite students to repeat the number after you. Pause after each group of ten (1–20, 21–30, 31–40, etc.) and then call out numbers at random within the group of ten.

### Shapes

Cut out a circle, rectangle, heart, square, triangle, and star. Ask students to name them with you.

## USING PAGE 2

Help students find page 2. Count from 21–100 and ask students to count with you. After students become familiar with the numbers, give commands such as: *Show me 21.* After students can identify the numbers, have students come up to the board to write different groups of ten (21–30, 31–40, etc.), saying each number as they write.

Help students find page 99 in their books. Do the numbers practice exercise with them.

## USING PAGE 3

Help students find page 3 in their books. Give the following directions:
*Find the circle. Color the circle brown. Find the star. Color the star orange. Find the triangle. Color the triangle yellow.*
*Find the rectangle. Color the rectangle green.*
*Find the square. Color the square blue.*
*Find the heart. Color the heart red.*

Help students find page 99 in their books. Do the shapes practice exercise with them.

# Seasons and Time

### Seasons

spring    summer

fall    winter

### Time

| 6:00 | 6:05 | 6:10 |
| --- | --- | --- |
| six o'clock | six-oh-five | six ten |

| 6:15 | 6:20 | 6:25 |
| --- | --- | --- |
| six fifteen | six twenty | six twenty-five |

| 6:30 | 6:35 | 6:40 |
| --- | --- | --- |
| six thirty | six thirty-five | six forty |

| 6:45 | 6:50 | 6:55 |
| --- | --- | --- |
| six forty-five | six fifty | six fifty-five |

**Vocabulary:** clock, fall, spring, summer, time, time from 1:00 to 12:00, winter

### Lesson Objectives
✓ to name and identify the four seasons
✓ to tell time

### Classroom English
• Find. Say. Listen. Write. Show me. Point to. Circle. What time is it?

### Language Patterns
• It is (spring).
• It is (6:55).

### Materials
paper plate; cardboard

## WARMING UP
### The Seasons

Invite students to join you at the window. Ask them to tell you what the weather is like and what season it is. Write the seasons on the board and read them with students.

### Time

Show students a clock you have made from a paper plate and cardboard. Move the hour hand around the clock as you say each hour. Ask students to say the hours with you. Move the minute hand and model the minutes as you count from 5 to 60 by fives. Ask students to count with you. Set the clock to 1:00. Say: *It's 1:00,* and ask students to repeat. Continue around the clock, moving the minute hand 5 minutes each time until you reach 2:00. Model these times and ask students to say them with you.

When students are familiar with telling time, set the clock to different times and ask: *What time is it?* Students respond: *It's (3:45).*

## USING PAGE 4

Help students find page 4 in their books. Ask them to find the current season. Point to the other seasons in the picture and ask students to repeat. Ask students to talk about what the weather is like in each picture. Talk about how seasons are different in other parts of the world. Help students find page 100 in their books. Do the seasons practice exercise.

## USING PAGE 5

Help students find page 5 in their books. Point to each clock and model the time. Ask students to say the time with you.

When students are comfortable telling time, help students find page 100 in their books. Do the time practice exercise.

# Imperatives and Hello!

**Vocabulary:** Be quiet. Close your book. Come here. Hello! Look at the board. Open your book. Please repeat. Raise your hand. Sit down. Stand up.

### Lesson Objectives
✓ to identify, say, and act out imperatives
✓ to greet others
✓ to tell others one's name

### Classroom English
• Find. Say. Listen. Write. Show me. Point to. Circle.

### Language Patterns
• Sit down.
• Stand up.
• Look at the board.
• (Open/Close) your book.
• Raise your hand.
• Come here.
• Be quiet.
• Please repeat.
• Hello!

### Materials
• crayons

## WARMING UP
### Imperatives

Use Total Physical Response (TPR) to introduce each command. Begin with: *Sit down. Stand up.* Introduce them together. Model the actions as you say the commands and ask students to do them with you. Write each command on the board and read them with students. You can also introduce the commands *Open your book.* and *Close your book.* together so students see the correlation between the opposites.

## USING PAGE 6

Help students find page 6 in their books. As you introduce all the commands, act them out for students and ask them to repeat the actions after you. Write the commands on the board and read them with students. You can introduce, reinforce, and practice commands as they come up during your lessons.

## USING PAGE 7
### Hello!

Help students find page 7 in their books. Read the speech bubbles and have students repeat. Role-play greetings with students. Invite a student to join you at the front of the class. Say: *Hello. My name is (Ms. Lewis).* Model the student's response and ask them to repeat: *Hello. My name is (Greg).* Give each student a chance to participate.

Have students find page 101 in their books. Explain to students that they should draw pictures of themselves in the space provided. Read the sentence at the bottom and ask students to read with you. Explain that they should write their names on the line. Pictures can be cut out of the book and displayed in the classroom.

# Unit 1
## My Class

### Contractions, Irregular Plurals

**Vocabulary:** close, cut, door, draw, glue, notebook, open, paper, picture, scissors, window

---

**Lesson Objectives**
✓ to identify classroom items
✓ to use verbs in the present progressive
✓ to use contractions with the verb *to be*

**Classroom English**
• Find. Say. Circle. Color. Draw. Write. Show me. What is it? What are you doing? What is (he/she) doing?

**Language Patterns**
• It is a (notebook).
• It is (glue).
• They are (scissors).

**Materials**
• Index cards with the letters: *I, a, m, y, o, u, a, r, e, h, l, s, s* and an apostrophe; crayons; markers; drawing paper; slips of paper with the words: *cut, glue, open, close, draw, paper, scissors*
• **Realia:** paper, scissors, glue, notebook
• **Picture Cards:** cut, open, close, draw, paper, scissors, glue, notebook

---

## WARMING UP

Show students realia or Picture Cards for *paper, scissors, glue,* and *notebook.* Introduce one word at a time. Ask students to repeat each word after you. Then use each word in a full sentence. Model and ask students to repeat: *It is a notebook. They are scissors.* Use Picture Cards to present the verbs: *cut, open, close, draw.*

After students are familiar with the nouns, give commands. Ask students to act out and say sentences with you: *Cut the paper. Close your notebook.*

Write the letters *I, a, m,* and an apostrophe on index cards. Form the words *I am.* Read the words with

**My Class**

window

door

notebook

glue

scissors

paper

picture

Contractions, Irregular Plurals  9

students. Take away the letter *a* and replace it with the apostrophe. Explain that we can sometimes make two words into one word by taking away letters and using an apostrophe. Use a similar procedure for the contractions *you're, he's, she's.*

Say sentences in the present progressive, using the contractions: *I'm opening the notebook.* Hold up the appropriate verb and noun Picture Cards as you say each sentence. Ask students to say the sentences with you and to act out the actions.

## USING PAGE 9

Help students find page 9 in their books. Allow students to talk about the pictures and encourage them to use

the key vocabulary from this unit. Play the recording or say the words as you point to each. Do a Show Me activity. Say sentences such as: *Show me paper. Show me a notebook.* Students point to the picture and say the words with you. Model complete sentences as students point to and say each new vocabulary word: *It is a notebook.*

Ask students to listen for directions as you say them:

*Find paper. Draw a red circle.*
*Find glue. Draw a purple circle.*
*Find picture. Draw a brown circle.*
*Find scissors. Draw a black circle.*

Help students find page 10 in their books. Play the recording or read the Grammar Box as you point to the pictures. Ask students to read with you. Explain that these actions are happening now. Explain how each contraction is formed.

Read the directions for the activity and ask students to read with you. Ask students to talk about what is happening in the picture. Say each sentence while pointing to the picture and ask students to say and point with you.

Read the first sentence with students. Read the words in parentheses. Explain that students will be writing contractions for the words in parentheses. Show students how to trace the first contraction and write the contractions for the other sentences. Students then find the picture that goes with each sentence and draw a line from the sentence to the picture. When they are finished, write the answers on the board and ask students to self-check their work.

## HAVING FUN!
### Contraction Match

Write these contractions and phrases on index cards: *I'm, You're, He's, She's, I am, You are, He is, She is.* You may want to make several sets so that more students can play. Read each index card aloud and then place all the index cards facedown on a table. Model the activity. Students take turns turning over two index cards. If they find a contraction that matches the full form, they keep the pair. Play until all the pairs are found. The student with the most pairs wins. Encourage students to use the contractions in sentences while playing.

### Forming Contractions

Ask students to write the following letters on index cards: *l, m, y, o, u, r,*

e, h, s, s. Students should also write an apostrophe on an index card. Say a contraction. Students use their index cards to form the contraction. The first student to correctly form the contraction gets a point. The student with the most points at the end of the game wins. Encourage students to use the contractions in sentences while playing.

You can also play a more difficult version of this game. Say the full form. Students use their index cards to form the contraction. For students with less English ability, write the contractions on the board to use as reference.

### Act It Out

Write the following words on slips of paper: *cut, glue, open, close, draw.*

Model the activity. Students come up, choose a slip of paper, and act out the verb. The rest of the class guesses what the action is. The student who guesses first gets to act out the next verb. Encourage students to guess using complete sentences that contain a contraction: *You're cutting paper. He's closing the notebook. She's gluing paper.*

**Vocabulary:** closing, cutting, door, drawing, gluing, notebook, opening, paper, picture, window

## Lesson Objectives
✓ to say and write sentences using the present progressive

✓ to use contractions with the verb *to be*

✓ to identify classroom objects

## Classroom English
• Find. Say. Circle. Color. Draw. Write. Show me. What is it? What are you doing? What is (he/she) doing?

## Language Patterns
• You're (cutting) (paper).
• They're (opening) a (notebook).
• We're (gluing) (paper).

## Materials
• Drawing paper, crayons, markers, two pieces of large poster board or paper, a pencil
• **Realia:** picture, paper, glue, notebook
• **Picture Cards:** scissors, paper, glue, notebook, cut, draw, open, close

Contractions, Irregular Plurals 11

## WARMING UP

Invite a group of students to come up and act out a sentence. Whisper the sentence: *You are cutting paper.* Ask the group to act it out. Invite the rest of the class to guess what they are doing. After the class has guessed, model the sentence: *They are cutting paper.* Write this sentence on the board and read it with students. Underline the words *They are* and write a new sentence using the contraction: *They're cutting paper.* Explain that you made a contraction for *They are* by taking out the letter *a* and replacing it with an apostrophe. Use a similar procedure for the contractions: *we're, you're.* When students are saying sentences with *we're,* point to yourself and the class. When students are saying sentences with *you're,* point to and talk to a few students.

Write the words: *they are, we are, you are* on the board and invite students to come up and help you change them to contractions. Display the Picture Cards: *cut, open, close, draw, paper, scissors, glue, notebook* on the board. Then write sentences with the full form on the board and ask volunteers to rewrite the sentences using a contraction. Students should point to the Picture Cards that go with the sentences. Model if necessary.

## 👀 USING PAGE 11

Help students find page 11 in their books. Ask students to tell what is happening in each picture. Play the recording or read the Grammar Box with students. Remind students that we can sometimes make two words

into one word by taking away one or more letters and replacing the letters with an apostrophe.

Read the directions for the activity and ask students to read with you. Ask students to tell what is happening in each picture. Read the first sentence and the words in parentheses. Explain that students will be writing contractions for these words. Show students how to trace the contraction in the first sentence. Then show them how to draw a line from the sentence to the matching picture. Complete the page with students. When students are finished, invite volunteers to read the sentences aloud. Write the answers on the board so students can self-check their work.

## USING PAGE 12

Help students find page 12 in their books. Ask students to tell what they see in the picture. Read the directions and ask students to follow along. Explain that they will be rewriting the sentences using a contraction and drawing a picture for each sentence. Read the first set of sentences and ask students to trace the sentence with the contraction. Complete the page with students. Write the sentences on the board as they are completed. When students are finished, ask volunteers to read each new sentence. Ask students to self-check their work.

## HAVING FUN!
### "What I Do at School" Books

Ahead of time, prepare an eight-page book using sentences with contractions. Students will make books about what they do in school. Show students the completed book. Ask them to tell what is happening in each picture. Give each student four pieces of drawing paper and show them how to fold the paper in half to make an eight-page book. Explain that they should draw pictures of what they do in school and then label them. Write key words on the board as reference: *cutting, gluing, paper, scissors.* Write one or two sentences on the board for students to use as reference: *I'm closing my notebook. You're closing the window.*

When students are finished, ask them to sit in a circle. Share your finished book with the class by pointing to the pictures and using simple language to talk about them. Use language from this unit such as: *I'm opening the notebook.* Invite volunteers to share their books with the rest of the class.

### Spin and Say a Sentence

Make a game board by drawing a large circle on a piece of poster board

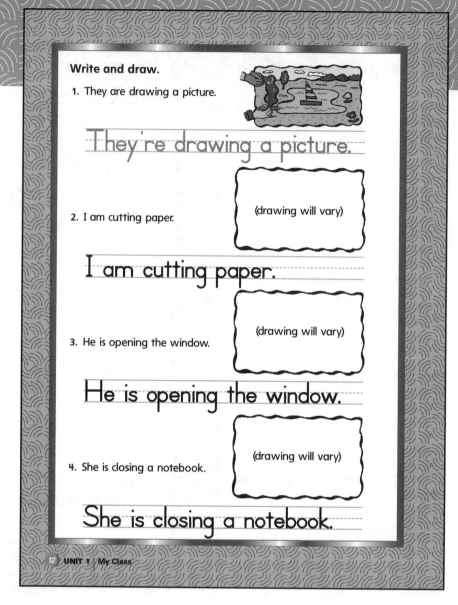

**Write and draw.**

1. They are drawing a picture.

They're drawing a picture.

2. I am cutting paper.

(drawing will vary)

I am cutting paper.

3. He is opening the window.

(drawing will vary)

He is opening the window.

4. She is closing a notebook.

(drawing will vary)

She is closing a notebook.

or large paper. Divide the circle into nine spaces. Write one word in each space: *cutting, gluing, opening, closing, drawing, paper, scissors, glue, notebook.* Model the activity. Place a pencil in the middle of the circle. Students take turns spinning the pencil. Students read the word and say a sentence in the present progressive for that word. Encourage students to use the contractions from this unit when saying their sentences.

### A Listening Game

Place the following Picture Cards on the board: *cut, opening, closing, drawing, paper, scissors, glue, notebook.* Ask students to form a line from the front to the back of the

room. Model the activity. Whisper a sentence to the first student using the vocabulary, a contraction, and the present progressive from this unit. For example: *I'm cutting paper.* Motion for the first student to whisper it to the next student in line. Students continue whispering the sentence until the last student is reached. The last student says the sentence and points to the corresponding Picture Cards on the board. The first student verifies if the sentence is correct. As students are playing, change their places in line so that each student gets a chance to be either the first or last in line. You may want to have more than one line to allow more students to participate at the same time.

**Vocabulary:** child, children, feet, foot, mice, mouse, teeth, tooth

**Lesson Objective**

✓ to say and write irregular plurals

**Classroom English**

• Find. Say. Circle. Color. Draw. Write. Show me. What is it? What are they?

**Language Patterns**

• It is a (tooth).

• They are (teeth).

**Materials**

• Index Cards with the words: *tooth, teeth, mouse, mice, foot, feet, child, children;* paper; crayons

• **Realia:** child, children, feet, foot

• Pictures or drawings of mice, a mouse; teeth, a tooth

## WARMING UP

Show students a picture for the word *tooth* and model the word for students. Ask students to say the word with you. Now show them a picture for the word *teeth.* Say the word and ask them to repeat. Explain that in English, some words do not use a final -s to form the plural. Instead, a new word is used. Use realia for the word pairs: *foot/feet, child/children.* Point to one of your feet, saying: *foot.* Point to both of your feet, saying: *feet.* Do a similar procedure for *child/children,* using your students as examples. Write each pair of words in two columns on the board and read them with students. Then mix up the plural forms and invite students to come up, find the plural for each singular noun, and draw a line from the singular to the plural word.

After students have practiced using the singular and plural forms of the irregular plurals, model sentences and ask them to repeat: *It is a tooth. They are teeth.* Write sentences using the singular and plural forms on the

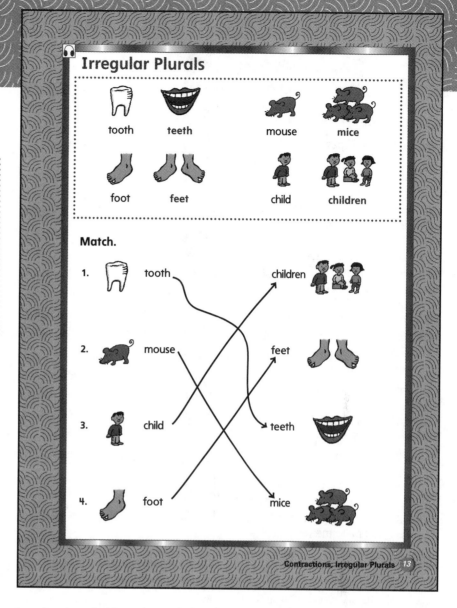

board and read with students. Explain that singular nouns use *is* and plural nouns use *are.*

## USING PAGE 13

Help students find page 13 in their books. Ask students to identify each picture using the singular and plural forms. Play the recording or read the Grammar Box with students. Remind students that some words do not take a final -s to form the plural. Instead, a different word is used.

Read the directions for the matching activity. Ask students to tell what they see in each picture. Explain that they will be matching the singular word to the plural word. Show students how to trace the line from the word *tooth*

to the word *teeth.* Complete the page with students. When finished, invite volunteers to read the singular and plural forms of each word. Write the answers on the board for students and ask them to self-check their work.

## Using Page 14

Help students find page 14 in their books. Ask them to tell what they see in each picture. Read the directions for Exercise A and ask students to read with you. Explain that they will be writing the plural form for each word. Read the words *foot* and *feet* with students. Show students how to trace the word *feet*. Read the word *child* in number 2. Ask students to tell you what the plural form is. Write the word *children* on the board for students to use as a reference as they complete number 2. Use a similar procedure for numbers 3 and 4.

Read the directions for Exercise B. Ask students to tell what they see in each picture. Read the first sentence with students and point out that there are two words at the end of each sentence. Tell students they have to choose the word that goes with the picture. Ask them to trace the circle around the word *mice* in the first sentence. Complete the rest of the page with students. Write the answers on the board for students and ask them to self-check their work.

When students are finished, invite volunteers to read each sentence for the rest of the class.

## Having Fun!
### Memory Game: Find the Pair

Write the following words on two separate sets of index cards: set 1: *tooth, mouse, child, foot;* set 2: *teeth, mice, children, feet.* You may want to make multiple sets so that more students can play at one time. Read each word with students and then place each index card facedown on the floor or on a table. Model the activity. Students turn over two index cards. If they get a singular/plural match they keep the pair. Play until all the pairs are found. The student with the most pairs at the end of the game wins. Encourage students to

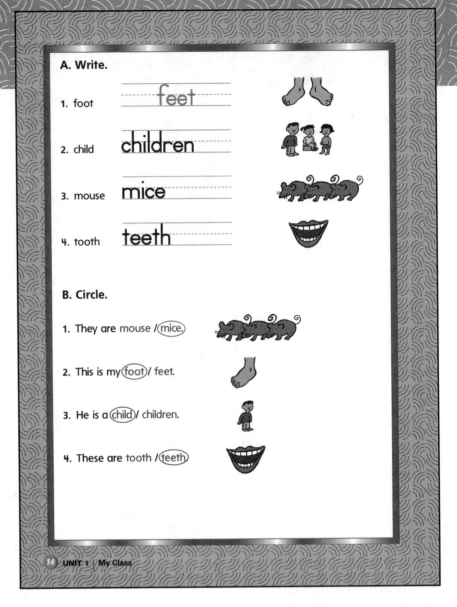

**A. Write.**

1. foot — *feet*
2. child — *children*
3. mouse — *mice*
4. tooth — *teeth*

**B. Circle.**

1. They are mouse /(mice.)
2. This is my (foot)/ feet.
3. He is a (child)/ children.
4. These are tooth /(teeth)

read the words and to use each word in a sentence.

### Word Bingo

Prepare Bingo grids with nine spaces for each student. Use paper clips or small pieces of paper for markers. Give each student a grid. Write the following words and draw a simple picture for each on the board: *tooth, teeth, mouse, mice, foot, feet, child, children.* Ask students to write the words and pictures in the spaces on their grid. Tell students that everyone's Bingo grid should be different. One space should be labeled *Free.* Play Bingo. Call out the words randomly. Students place markers on the word and picture you say. Three in a row wins. The winner reads the words in

the winning row aloud and uses each word in a sentence.

### A Guessing Game

Place pictures of the following in a pile: *foot, feet, child, children, mouse, mice, tooth, teeth.* (You might want to include *man/men* and *woman/women* if you have taught these forms.) Cover the top picture with a piece of paper. Tell students to watch carefully while you lift the paper very slowly. As you lift the paper, students guess what picture is on top. Continue playing until students guess all the pictures. As students guess, encourage them to use complete sentences: *It's a foot. They are feet.*

**Vocabulary:** closing, cutting, door, drawing, gluing, notebook, opening, paper, picture, window

### Lesson Objectives
✓ to name classroom objects
✓ to use sentences in the present progressive
✓ to use contractions with the verb *to be*

### Classroom English
• Draw. Show me. Find. Say. What is it? What is this? What are they?

### Language Patterns
• I'm (closing) a (book).
• (He's/She's) (cutting) (paper).
• They're (drawing).
• You're (gluing).

### Materials
• Crayons and pencils or markers, poster board, magazines
• **Picture Cards:** cut, open, close, draw, paper, scissors, notebook

## WARMING UP

Begin by reviewing the vocabulary and present progressive from this unit. Review the contractions: *he's, she's, you're, I'm, we're, they're.* Remind students how each contraction is formed.

Ask students to take turns role-playing the actions as you say sentences such as: *He's drawing a picture. She's cutting paper.*

##  USING PAGE 15

Help students find page 15 in their books. Play the recording or read the chant aloud. Act out each action as it is said in the chant. Model and ask students to follow along and point to each word as they listen. After students have listened to and read the chant a few times, invite them to say it with you. Encourage them

**🎧 Chant.**

He's drawing a picture.
He is.
He is.

She's gluing the pictures.
She is.
She is.

You're closing a window.
You are.
You are.

I'm cutting paper.
I am.
I am.

Contractions, Irregular Plurals (15)

to point to each word as they read and to act out the actions with you. Model as necessary.

## EXTENSION
### Continue the Chant

Review the chant with students by playing the recording or reading it aloud. Substitute other actions and classroom objects. Students say the new chant and act out the new activity or action. Invite volunteers to come up and point to the corresponding Picture Cards as they are said in the chant.

### Take the Parts

Divide the class into two groups. One group says the first sentence with the

contraction. The second group says the short sentences that do not have contractions.

### A Mural of Our Classroom

Provide students with a large piece of poster board or use the plain side of a long piece of wallpaper. Explain that students will be making a mural of their classroom and all the things and people in it. Model what is to be done. Students can draw pictures or cut out pictures from magazines to create their mural. When they are finished, invite individuals to come up and identify the items they have included. Model vocabulary such as *They are children. It is a door.* Display the mural in the hallway or classroom for everyone to enjoy.

**Vocabulary:** closing, cutting, door, drawing, glue, gluing, notebook, opening, paper, picture, window

### Lesson Objectives
✓ to name classroom objects

✓ to identify actions

✓ to use sentences in the present progressive

✓ to use contractions with the verb *to be*

### Classroom English
• Draw. Show me. Find. Say. What is it? What is this? What are they?

### Language Patterns
• I'm (closing) a (book).

• (He's/She's) (cutting) (paper).

• They're (drawing).

• You're (gluing).

### Materials
• Crayons and pencils or markers

• **Realia:** door, window, paper, scissors, glue, notebook

• **Picture Cards:** cut, open, close, draw, paper, scissors, glue, notebook

---

**Find the differences.**

1.

2.

## WARMING UP

Review the vocabulary and the present progressive from this unit. Use realia or hold up each Picture Card and ask students to identify it using a complete sentence. For example: *It is a notebook.*

Write the verbs on the board and read them with students. Invite students to come up and match the verb to the Picture Card. Invite students to use the verb Picture Cards and the noun Picture Cards to make sentences. For example: *He's drawing a picture. I'm cutting paper.*

## USING PAGE 16

Help students find page 16 in their books. Ask students to tell what they see in the first picture. Then ask students to tell what each child is doing

in the picture. Encourage them to use sentences such as: *He's gluing paper. She's closing a window.* Now ask students to look at the second picture and to tell what they see and what each person is doing. Point out that the pictures are different. Invite students to tell how the pictures are not the same. For example: *In picture 1, the girl is closing the window. In picture 2, the girl is opening the window.* When they are finished, ask students to talk about them with a partner. They can discuss what each person is doing and how the actions are different.

## EXTENSION
### Information Gap Activity

Model the activity. Ask students to sit back-to-back with their books. Student 1 picks a picture and places a marker

on it. Student 2 guesses which picture it is by saying a sentence in the present progressive: *He is drawing.* Student 2 continues guessing until he or she guesses correctly. Students then change roles and play again.

### Draw

Give each student a piece of drawing paper and show them how to fold it in half like a book. Explain that they will be drawing pictures that are similar to the ones in their Student Book (but simpler, with less detail). Explain that the pictures should have some similar things and some different things. When they are finished, ask students to switch papers with a partner. Each student then tries to find the differences in their partner's drawings.

# Unit 2
## On the Playground

### Prepositions, *There is/There are, How many...?*

**Vocabulary:** above, ant, behind, bench, butterfly, cloud, flower, next to, seesaw, squirrel, sun, swing, tree

**Lesson Objectives**
✓ to identify items on the playground
✓ to identify animals and insects

**Classroom English**
- Find. Say. Circle. Color. Draw. Write. Show me. What is it? It is (a/an) (ant/tree).

**Language Patterns**
- It is a (tree).
- It is an (ant).

**Materials**
- Crayons, markers, drawing paper, slips of paper with the words: *tree, sun, cloud, bench, swing, seesaw, flower, squirrel, butterfly, ant*
- **Picture Cards:** tree, sun, cloud, bench, swing, seesaw, flower, squirrel, butterfly, ant

### WARMING UP

Show students Picture Cards for *tree, sun, cloud, bench, swing, seesaw, flower, squirrel, butterfly,* and *ant*. Model each word by holding up the Picture Card and saying it for students. Introduce one word at a time. After students are familiar with the new vocabulary, place the Picture Cards on the floor or table in front of them. Play a Show Me game. Say: *Show me (a flower). Show me (an ant).* Invite students to come up and point to the card you named. Then ask them to say the word.

Model sentences with the new vocabulary as you hold up each Picture Card: *It is (a seesaw). It is (an ant).* Invite students to say the sentences with you.

 ### USING PAGE 17

Help students find page 17 in their books. Play the recording or read each

word as you point to it. Ask students to point and repeat after you. Repeat using complete sentences: *It is (an ant). It is (a flower).*

### HAVING FUN!
#### Act It Out

Model an action for each word. Write each word on a separate slip of paper and place the words in a bag or box. Invite students to choose a word and act it out for the rest of the class. The student who guesses first gets to act out the next word.

#### Drawing Dictation

Distribute paper and crayons to students. Show students how to fold a piece of drawing paper so there are eight spaces. Give directions for

students to draw the objects using the correct colors. Model the activity if necessary.

*Draw a green tree.*
*Draw a yellow sun.*
*Draw a white cloud.*
*Draw a brown bench.*
*Draw a red swing.*
*Draw a green seesaw.*
*Draw a purple flower.*
*Draw a brown bench.*
*Draw a blue butterfly.*
*Draw a red ant.*

After students have finished, ask them to talk about the pictures.

**Vocabulary:** above, ant, behind, bench, butterfly, cloud, flower, next to, seesaw, squirrel, sun, swing, tree

### Lesson Objectives
✓ to identify items on the playground

✓ to identify animals and insects

✓ to use prepositions of place

### Classroom English
• Find. Say. Circle. Color. Draw. Write. Show me. What is it? Where is the (cloud)?

### Language Patterns
• It is a (cloud).

• It is an (ant).

• The (cloud) is (behind) the (sun).

### Materials
• Drawing paper, crayons, markers, glue, a bag or box, one set of Picture Cards for each student

• **Picture Cards:** tree, sun, cloud, bench, swing, seesaw, flower, squirrel, butterfly, ant

## WARMING UP

Bring in a large box or bag. Use realia in your classroom or the Picture Cards from this unit. Place one of the Picture Cards *next to* the bag or box and model the preposition *next to*. Ask students to repeat. Now model a prepositional phrase and ask students to say it with you: *next to the (bag)*. Model the sentence: *The (ant) is next to the (bag)*. Continue with additional examples that allow students to practice the preposition *next to*. Use a similar procedure for the prepositions *behind* and *above*.

Write the following sentences on the board:

*Draw a cloud.*
*Draw a sun above the cloud.*
*Draw a tree.*
*Draw a flower next to the tree.*
*Draw a squirrel behind the tree.*

---

## Prepositions: behind, next to, above

The cloud is behind the sun.

The cloud is next to the sun.

The cloud is above the sun.

### Read and draw.

1. The sun is above the cloud.

2. The tree is next to the flower.

3. The butterfly is above the ant.

4. The squirrel is behind the tree.

(drawings will vary)

---

Read the sentences with students and invite individuals to come up to the board and draw pictures for each sentence. As students are drawing, ask them to tell where they are drawing each item. Invite students to add sentences to the list and to draw additional items. Leave the pictures on the board.

Write the following words on the board: *sun/the/is/above/cloud/the.* Read the words with students and ask them to make a sentence that talks about a picture from the board. Model if necessary. Write the sentence on the board and read it with the class. Continue the activity by writing other words in random order and asking students to create sentences about a picture.

##  USING PAGE 18

Help students find page 18 in their books. Ask them to tell where the items in each picture are. Play the recording or read the Grammar Box with students. Explain that the words *behind, next to,* and *above* are prepositions that tell us where things and people are in relation to each other.

Read the directions for the activity and ask students to read with you. Tell students to draw a picture for each sentence. Complete the page with students. When they are finished, invite individuals to identify the items and to tell where they are.

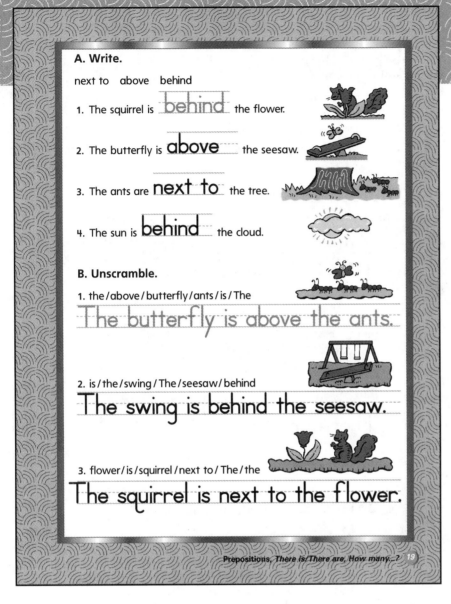

**A. Write.**

next to   above   behind

1. The squirrel is **behind** the flower.

2. The butterfly is **above** the seesaw.

3. The ants are **next to** the tree.

4. The sun is **behind** the cloud.

**B. Unscramble.**

1. the / above / butterfly / ants / is / The

The butterfly is above the ants.

2. is / the / swing / The / seesaw / behind

The swing is behind the seesaw.

3. flower / is / squirrel / next to / The / the

The squirrel is next to the flower.

## Prepositions Commands

Make a set of Picture Cards for each student. Give commands that use the prepositions *next to, above,* and *behind.* For example: *Find the squirrel. Find the flower. Put the squirrel behind the flower.* As students place their Picture Cards in the correct spots, invite them to tell where the items are. Model sentences if necessary.

## Information Gap Activity

Model the activity. Students play in pairs. Each student should have one set of Picture Cards. Student 1 chooses two Picture Cards and asks Student 2 to guess which pictures they are: *What are my pictures?* Student 1 then arranges the pictures so that he or she is demonstrating one of the prepositions *next to, above,* or *behind.* Student 2 guesses where the items are by saying a sentence: *The (squirrel) is (next to) the (tree).* After Student 2 guesses correctly, he or she looks at his or her partner's Picture Cards. Students change roles and play again.

## USING PAGE 19

Help students find page 19 in their books. Read the directions and ask students to read with you. Read the words at the top of the exercise. Ask students to talk about where things are in each picture. Explain that students will be completing the sentences using prepositions. Read the sentence in number 1. Show students how to trace the preposition *behind.* Complete the exercise with students. Write the prepositions on the board and ask students to self-check their work.

Read the directions for the next activity and ask students to read with you. Read the words in number 1. Ask students to trace the sentence in number 1. Ask students to talk about

the pictures and to use the words to write a sentence about each one. When students are finished, write the answers on the board and ask them to self-check their work.

## HAVING FUN!
### Listen for Directions

Ask students to stand next to a chair, table, or box. Give Total Physical Response (TPR) commands that use the prepositions *next to, above,* and *behind.* For example, *Stand next to your chair. Put your hand above your chair. Stand behind your chair.* Model if necessary. As students act out the commands, ask them to tell where they are by using the prepositions: *I am next to the chair.*

**Vocabulary:** ant(s), bench(es), butterfly(ies), cloud(s), flower(s), seesaw(s), squirrel(s), sun(s), swing(s), tree(s)

**Lesson Objectives**
✓ to use singular and plural nouns
✓ to use *there is* and *there are* for singular and plural nouns
✓ to use prepositions to tell where items are

**Classroom English**
• Find. Say. Write. What is this?

**Language Patterns**
• There is a (cloud) (in front of) the (sun).
• There are (flowers) (behind) the (tree).

**Materials**
• **Picture Cards:** tree, sun, cloud, bench, swing, seesaw, flower, squirrel, butterfly, ant

## WARMING UP

Make multiple copies of the Picture Cards. Show students a single item and model the word. Ask students to repeat. Show students more than one of the same item and model the plural form. Emphasize the final *-s*. Ask students to repeat. Use a similar procedure for the rest of the vocabulary words. Write the words on the board and read them with students. Point out the irregular spellings for *butterflies* and *benches*. Students should not be expected to produce these irregular plurals at this time.

Hold up one of the Picture Cards and place it *(next to)* one of the other Picture Cards. Model a sentence using a preposition and *there is*. For example: *There is an (ant) (next to) the (bench).* Ask students to repeat. Give other examples for students and ask them to say the sentences with you.

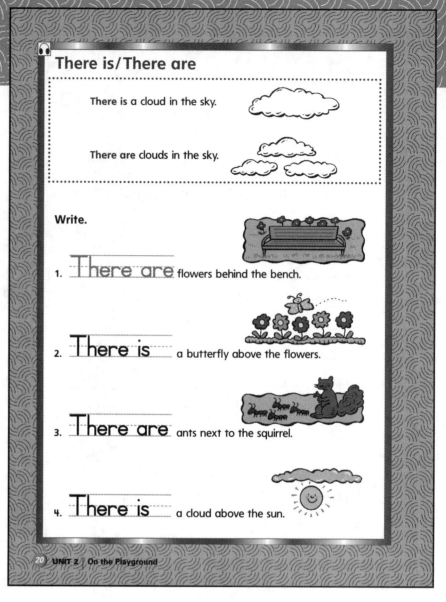

Now show students more than one of the same Picture Card and ask them to tell what they see. Place these Picture Cards *(behind)* another Picture Card. Model the sentence *There are (benches) (behind) the (tree).* Ask students to repeat after you.

## USING PAGE 20

Help students find page 20 in their books. Ask them to identify each picture using the singular and plural forms. Play the recording or read the Grammar Box with students. Explain that we use *there is* for one item or person and *there are* for more than one item or person.

Read the directions for the activity. Ask students to tell what they see in each picture. Explain that they will be writing either *there is* or *there are* to complete the sentences. Ask students to read the first sentence with you and to trace the words *There are*.

## HAVING FUN!
### Change It

Make multiple copies of the Picture Cards. Model the activity. Hold up one *cloud* and the *sun*. Place the *cloud* in front of the *sun*. Say: *There is one cloud in front of the sun.* Then change the sentence to: *There are clouds in front of the sun.* Hold up more than one cloud and place it in front of the *sun* Picture Card. Continue the activity by saying sentences with one item and asking students to change the sentences to plurals.

**Vocabulary:** ant, bench, butterfly, cloud, flower, seesaw, squirrel, sun, swing, tree

### Lesson Objectives
✓ to identify items on the playground
✓ to ask and tell how many items there are
✓ to use *there is* and *there are* to talk about singular and plural items

### Classroom English
• Find. Say. Circle. Color. Draw. Write. Show me. What is it? What are they? Where is the (bench)?

### Language Patterns
• How many (flowers) are there?
• There are (five) flowers.
• There is (one) flower.

### Materials
• Index Cards with the numerals and words: *one–ten*; one Bingo grid and markers for each student; drawing paper; markers; crayons
• **Picture Cards:** tree, sun, cloud, bench, swing, seesaw, flower, squirrel, butterfly, ant

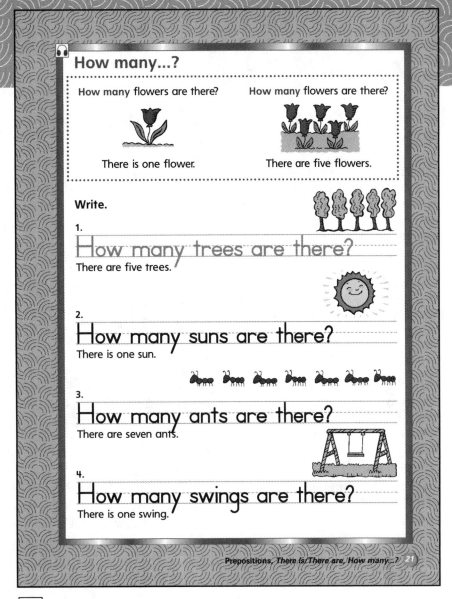

## How many...?

How many flowers are there?

There is one flower.

How many flowers are there?

There are five flowers.

**Write.**

1.

How many trees are there?

There are five trees.

2.

How many suns are there?

There is one sun.

3.

How many ants are there?

There are seven ants.

4.

How many swings are there?

There is one swing.

Prepositions, *There is/There are, How many...?* 21

## WARMING UP

Use multiple copies of the Picture Cards. Hold up *(three) (ants)* and ask students to count them. Then ask: *How many (ants) are there?* Model the response: *There are three ants.* Ask students to repeat both the question and the answer. Continue the activity with additional examples.

Invite a student to come up. Whisper the sentence: *There (are) (two) (trees).* Ask him or her to pick up the correct number of the item. *How many (trees) (are) there?* Tell the class to ask the question to the student. The student then replies: *There are (two) (trees).* Continue the activity. Write the questions and responses on the board. Invite students to read with you.

## 🎧 USING PAGE 21

Help students find page 21 in their books. Ask them to identify each picture using the singular and plural forms. Play the recording or read the Grammar Box with students. Explain that when we want to know how many, we say: *How many (seesaws) are there?* Remind students that we use *there is* for one item or person and *there are* for more than one item or person.

Read the directions for the activity. Ask students to tell what they see in each picture. Explain that they will be writing questions about the pictures. Read the first question and response with students and ask them to trace the question. Use a similar procedure to complete the page with students.

## USING PAGE 22

Help students find page 22 in their books. Read the directions with students. Read the first question and response. Explain that students will be finishing the questions by writing *How many* and completing the responses by writing either *There is* or *There are.* Ask students to trace the words *How many* and *There is* in number 1. Complete each question and answer with students and write the answers on the board so students can self-check their work.

When students are finished writing, ask them to draw a picture that illustrates each sentence they just completed. Draw a picture on the board as students are working so they can use it as a reference.

## HAVING FUN!
### Numeral and Number Word Match

Write the numerals 1–10 on one set of cards. Write the number words *one* through *ten* on another set of cards. You may want to make multiple sets of cards so that more students can play at one time. Begin by asking students to count from one to ten as you hold up each numeral. Then mix up the order and ask students to identify each numeral.

Show students the number words and read them with students. Begin by reading them in order and then mix them up. Place the numeral and number word index cards on the floor or on a table in front of students. Students take turns turning over two cards. If students find a match, they keep the pair. The student with the most pairs at the end of the game wins. As students are playing, encourage them to identify the numerals and read the number words.

### Ask *How Many?*

Use multiple copies of the same Picture Cards. Invite one student to

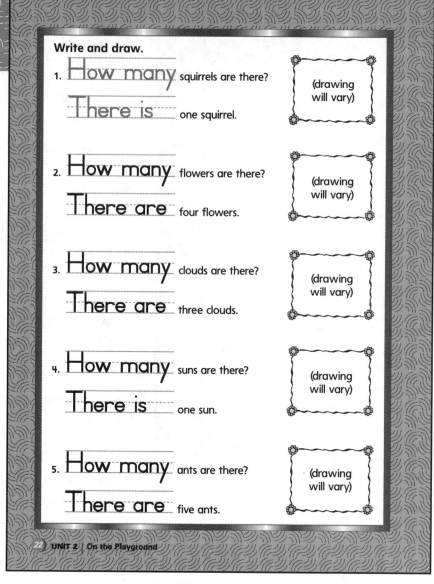

**Write and draw.**

1. How many squirrels are there?
   There is one squirrel. (drawing will vary)

2. How many flowers are there?
   There are four flowers. (drawing will vary)

3. How many clouds are there?
   There are three clouds. (drawing will vary)

4. How many suns are there?
   There is one sun. (drawing will vary)

5. How many ants are there?
   There are five ants. (drawing will vary)

22 UNIT 2 | On the Playground

come up while the rest of the class closes their eyes. The student chooses any amount from one to ten of one of the Picture Cards. The student places the Picture Cards behind his or her back. After he or she has finished, the rest of the class opens their eyes. The student up front asks: *How many (trees) are there?* Students then take turns guessing how many *(trees)* the student has. The student who guesses correctly counts the items and then chooses the next set of items.

### Drawing Dictation

Show students how to fold their paper into eight spaces. Dictate sentences and ask students to draw pictures that illustrate your sentences:

1. *There are three clouds.*
2. *There are four flowers.*
3. *There is one sun.*
4. *There are five squirrels.*
5. *There are two ants.*
6. *There are seven butterflies.*
7. *There are two seesaws.*
8. *There are six swings.*

When students have finished, ask them either to write the number word under the picture or to write a sentence about the picture using *There is/are* plus a numeral. Model if necessary. Then ask students to share their work with the rest of the class.

**Vocabulary:** above, ant, behind, bench, butterfly, cloud, flower, next to, seesaw, squirrel, sun, swing, tree

### Lesson Objectives
✓ to name items on the playground
✓ to identify animals and insects
✓ to tell how many items there are
✓ to use prepositions to tell where items are

### Classroom English
• Show me. Find. Say. What is it? What is this? What are they? Where is the (flower)?

### Language Patterns
• There is a (cloud).
• There are (benches).
• The (flower) is (next to) the (bench).

### Materials
• **Picture Cards:** tree, sun, cloud, bench, swing, seesaw, flower, squirrel, butterfly

## WARMING UP

Begin by reviewing the playground, animal, and insect words with students. Hold up more than one of the same Picture Card and ask: *How many (trees) are there?* Ask students to respond and model if necessary.

Review the prepositions *next to, above, behind.* Hold up two Picture Cards and place them according to one of the prepositions. Ask students to tell where the object is. Model responses if necessary.

 ## USING PAGE 23

Help students find page 23 in their books. Play the recording or read the chant aloud. Use the Picture Cards to illustrate the sentences in the chant. Ask students to follow along and point to each word as they listen. After students have listened to and read the chant a few times, invite them to say it with you. Encourage students to point to each word as

Chant.

There is an ant.
Where's the ant?
The ant is next to the tree.
The ant is next to the tree.

There is a sun.
Where's the sun?
The sun is above the cloud.
The sun is above the cloud.

There is a squirrel.
Where's the squirrel?
The squirrel is behind the bench.
The squirrel is behind the bench.

There is a flower.
Where's the flower?
The flower is next to the swing.
The flower is next to the swing.

Prepositions, *There is/There are, How many...?* 23

they read. Model as necessary. Place the corresponding Picture Cards on the board. Say the chant again and invite students to come up and point to the corresponding Picture Cards as they hear them in the chant.

## EXTENSION
### Continue the Chant

Review the chant with students by playing the recording or reading it aloud. Substitute other prepositions, playground words, insects, and animals. Invite volunteers to come up and point to the corresponding Picture Cards as they hear them in the chant.

### Take the Parts

Divide the class into two groups. Group 1 can say lines 1, 3, and 4. Group 2 can ask the question in line 2. After students have said the chant, ask them to change parts.

**Vocabulary:** above, ant, behind, bench, butterfly, cloud, flower, next to, seesaw, squirrel, sun, swing, tree

**Lesson Objectives**
✓ to name items on the playground
✓ to identify animals and insects
✓ to tell how many items there are
✓ to use prepositions to tell where items are

**Classroom English**
• Show me. Find. Say. What is it? What is this? What are they? Where is the (flower)?

**Language Patterns**
• There is a (cloud).
• There are (benches).
• The flower is (next to) the (bench).

**Materials**
• Crayons, pencils, markers
• **Picture Cards:** tree, sun, cloud, bench, swing, seesaw, flower, squirrel, butterfly

## WARMING UP

Tape the Picture Cards on the board in an *S* pattern. Use your finger to follow the pattern and name each Picture Card as you pass over it. Invite students to come up and repeat the activity. Model words if necessary.

Repeat the activity, but use complete sentences as you pass each word. For example: *It's a seesaw.*

Now tape the Picture Cards in two rows. Ask questions about where the Picture Cards are. For example: *Where is the butterfly?* Ask students to respond and model responses if necessary: *The butterfly is above the seesaw.*

## USING PAGE 24

Help students find page 24 in their books. Ask students to tell what they see in the picture. Explain that the

**Find the flower.**

butterfly is looking for the flower and that they should help the butterfly by completing the maze. Explain that they cannot cross any lines to get to the end. Students can work in pairs to complete the maze. When they are finished, ask students to tell what pictures they pass as they trace the path in the maze.

### Extension

Students draw their own mazes and exchange them with another student to complete.

# Units 1 & 2
## Review

**Vocabulary:** ant, bench, butterfly, close, cloud, cut, draw, door, flower, glue, notebook, open, paper, scissors, seesaw, squirrel, sun, swing, tree, window

### Review Objectives
✓ to identify classroom items
✓ to identify items on the playground
✓ to identify animals and insects
✓ to identify prepositions of place
✓ to identify questions with *How many?* and answers with *There is/are*

### Classroom English
• Listen. Check. Point. Say.

### Language Patterns
• (It is/It's) a (window).
• There are (three) (clouds).
• The (cloud) is (above) the (sun).
• How many (trees) are there?
• There is one (sun).

### Materials
• a large box
• **Realia:** paper, scissors, glue, notebook, flower
• **Picture Cards:** cut, open, close, draw, paper, scissors, glue, notebook, tree, sun, cloud, bench, swing, seesaw, flower, squirrel, butterfly, ant

## WARMING UP

Use realia or Picture Cards to review the nouns and verbs from Units 1 and 2. Encourage students to say what they can.

Bring in a large box and stand inside the box. Say: *I'm in the box.* Stand

---

## Review: Units 1 and 2

### Vocabulary
🎧 **A. Listen and check.**

### There is/There are
🎧 **B. Listen and check.**

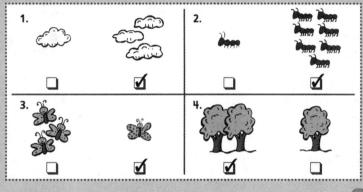

Review | Units 1 and 2 ㉕

---

next to the box and say: *I'm next to the box.* Repeat for the prepositions *behind* and *above.* Invite students to come up and act out commands. For example: *Stand in the box. Put the pencil above the box.*

Place the following Picture Cards on the board: *cloud, sun, bench, swing, seesaw, flower, tree.* Place the cloud above the tree and say: *The cloud is above the tree.* Present additional examples using the prepositions *behind, above, in, on.* Give directions using prepositions and invite students

to place the Picture Cards: *Put the (bench) (next to) the (tree).*

Draw an outline of a simple playground on the board. Place the Unit 2 Picture Cards in the playground. Model sentences such as: *There is a (bench) on the playground. There are (trees) in the playground.* Invite students to say sentences about the playground using *There is* and *There are.* Model additional sentences if necessary.

Make multiple copies of the Unit 2 Picture Cards. Count the pictures with

---

## AUDIOSCRIPT

**A.** 1. flower     2. window     3. swing     4. tree

**B.** 1. There are three clouds.     2. There are seven ants.     3. There is one butterfly.     4. There are two trees.

students and ask: *How many (trees) are there?* Model the response: *There are (five) (trees).* Provide additional examples for students that allow them to count and use *There is* and *There are* to show how many.

Tape two different Picture Cards to the board and draw a small box under each one. Say *(It's/It is) a (tree).* Point to each Picture Card and ask students to tell you which card matches your sentence. Invite a student to place a check in the correct box. Provide additional examples and invite students to come up and check the correct boxes.

If you feel students need to practice exercises that are similar to those presented in the Review Units, use exercises like the previous one. You can use similar exercises for any of the Review Exercises at the end of each unit.

## USING PAGE 25

Help students find page 25 in their books. Help students find Exercise A. Read the directions and ask students to follow along. Point to each picture and ask students to say the words with you. Explain to students that they should check the picture that goes with the word they hear. Play the recording or read the audioscript. Students check the correct picture.

Help students find Exercise B. Read the directions and ask them to follow along. Point to the picture and ask students to repeat each word after you. Explain to students that they should check the picture that goes

### Prepositions
🎧 C. Listen and check.

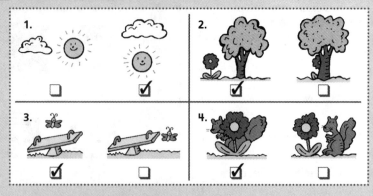

🎧 **How many...?**
D. Listen, point, and say.

26   Review | Units 1 and 2

with the sentence they hear. Play the recording or read the audioscript. Students check the correct picture.

## USING PAGE 26

Help students find page 26 in their books. Help students find Exercise C. Read the directions and ask students to follow along. Point to the pictures and ask students to tell you where each item is. Explain to students that

they should check the picture that goes with the sentence they hear. Play the recording or read the audioscript. Students check the correct picture.

Help students find Exercise D. Read the directions and ask students to follow along. Explain that they should listen, find, and point to the corresponding picture, and then say the question and answer. Play the recording or read the audioscript.

---

### AUDIOSCRIPT

**C.** 1. The cloud is above the sun.
3. The butterfly is above the seesaw.

2. The flower is next to the tree.
4. The squirrel is behind the flower.

**D.** 1. How many suns are there? There is one sun.
3. How many flowers are there? There are three flowers.

2. How many seesaws are there? There is one seesaw.
4. How many trees are there? There are two trees.

# Unit 3
## Our House

### Possessives, *Is there...?/Are there...?*

**Vocabulary:** bike, computer, door, house, mirror, pet, radio, rug, sink, telephone, window

**Lesson Objectives**
✓ to identify items in a house
✓ to use possessives *my* and *yours*

**Classroom English**
• Find. Say. Circle. Color. Draw. Write. Show me. What is (this/that)? (This/That) is a (sink).

**Language Patterns**
• This is a (window).
• That is a (bike).

**Materials**
• Crayons, markers, drawing paper, slips of paper with the words: *house, door, window, telephone, radio, mirror, sink, pet, rug, computer, bike*
• **Picture Cards:** house, door, room, window, telephone, radio, mirror, sink, pet, rug, computer, bike

### WARMING UP

Show students Picture Cards for *house, window, door, room, telephone, radio, mirror, sink, pet, rug, computer,* and *bike*. Introduce one word at a time. Ask students to repeat the words after you say each one. Then use each word in a full sentence. Model and ask students to repeat: *This is a (telephone).* Review the use of *this* and *that.* Hold one of the Picture Cards in your hand and say: *This is a (mirror).* Place the Picture Card far away and say: *That is a (mirror).* Remind students that we use *this* when something or someone is close to us. We use *that* when things or people are far away from us.

After students are familiar with the nouns, do a Show Me activity. Place the Picture Cards on the floor or on a table in front of students. Say: *Show me the (telephone).* Invite individual students to come up and point to the

correct picture. Encourage them to tell what it is and to use a complete sentence: *This is a radio.*

Draw a picture of your house ahead of time and show it to students. Point to the picture and say: *This is my house.* Now give students a piece of drawing paper and ask them to draw pictures of their houses. When they are finished, model the sentence: *This is my house.* Invite students to hold up their pictures and to say the sentence with you.

Ask students to sit in pairs. Invite one student to be your partner. Point and say: *This is your house.* Emphasize the word *your.* Motion for students to point to their partners' pictures and to repeat the sentence. Invite students to circulate and to identify their

houses by saying: *This is my house* and to identify their classmates' houses by saying: *This is your house.*

Explain that when something belongs to you, you use the word *my.* When something belongs to another person, you use the word *your.*

### 🎧 USING PAGE 27

Help students find page 27 in their books. Play the recording or read each word as you point to it. Allow students to talk about the picture and encourage them to use the key vocabulary from this unit. As you name each word, point to the pictures. Ask students to point with you. Model complete sentences for students and ask students to repeat as you point to the pictures: *This is a (window).*

## 🎧 USING PAGE 28

Help students find page 28 in their books. Play the recording or read the Grammar Box as you point to the pictures. Ask students to read with you. Explain that we use the word *my* when something belongs to us. We use the word *your* when something belongs to someone else.

Read the directions for the activity and ask students to follow along. Model sentences and ask students to talk about what is happening in the pictures: *This is my computer. That is your computer.* Remind students that we use *this* for items that are close to us. We use *that* for items that are far away. Read the first sentence and ask students to trace the word *my*. Help students find the matching picture and ask them to draw a line from the picture to the sentence. Complete the page with students. Students fill in the possessives *my* and *your* and match the sentence to the picture. Write the answers on the board and ask students to self-check their work.

## HAVING FUN!
### Drawing Dictation

Give each student a piece of drawing paper and show them how to fold it into eight spaces. Students draw eight pictures on the front and three pictures on the back. Students can number the spaces 1–11. Give the following directions and draw pictures with students so they have a better understanding of the activity.

*Draw a house.*
*Draw a window.*
*Draw a door.*
*Draw a telephone.*
*Draw a radio.*
*Draw a mirror.*
*Draw a sink.*
*Draw a pet.*
*Draw a rug.*
*Draw a computer.*
*Draw a bike.*

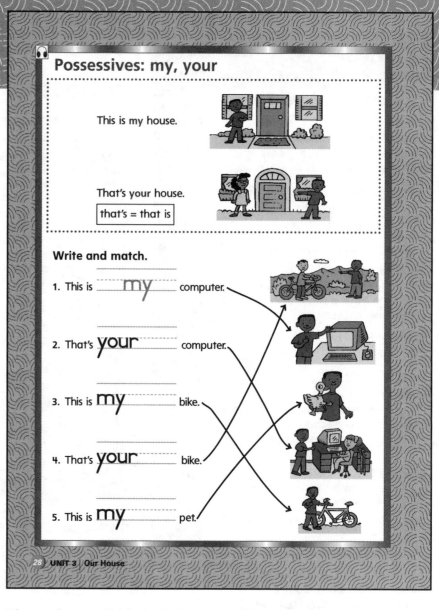

### Possessives: my, your

This is my house.

That's your house.

that's = that is

**Write and match.**

1. This is ___my___ computer.

2. That's **your** computer.

3. This is **my** bike.

4. That's **your** bike.

5. This is **my** pet.

When students are finished, ask them to work in pairs. Students take turns pointing to their pictures and their partner's pictures and saying: *This is (my) computer. That is (your) computer.*

### Act It Out

Write the following words on slips of paper and read them with students: *house, door, window, telephone, radio, mirror, sink, pet, rug, computer, bike.* As you read each word, use a gesture or act out using the item. Fold and place the slips of paper in a bag or box. Invite students to come up, choose a slip of paper, read it, and then act it out. The student who guesses first gets to be the next actor.

### This Is Your Picture

Ask students to draw a picture of their house. Students should not write their names on the pictures. Encourage students to work independently so they can play a guessing game with the pictures. Collect the finished pictures and randomly hand them out. Model the activity. Students circulate and try to find the student who drew the picture. Encourage them to say: *This is your house.* If a student says *no*, the questioning student moves on to another student until the owner of the picture is found.

**Vocabulary:** bike, computer, door, house, mirror, pet, radio, rug, sink, telephone, window

### Lesson Objectives
✓ to identify items in a house
✓ to form possessives by adding 's to the end of a name
✓ to use the possessives *my, our,* and *your*

### Classroom English
• Find. Say. Circle. Color. Draw. Write. Show me. What is it? This is a (bike).

### Language Patterns
• This is (Taro's) bike.
• That's (Matt's) house.
• (This/That) is (my/our/your) (house).

### Materials
• Drawing paper, crayons, markers, index cards with students' names, one set of Picture Cards for each student, index cards with the words: *house, door, window, telephone, radio, mirror, sink, pet, rug, computer, bike*
• **Picture Cards:** house, door, window, telephone, radio, mirror, sink, pet, rug, computer, bike

---

## Possessives: -'s

That's Matt's house.

**Write and match.**

1. That's ___Taro's___ bike.
   (Taro)

2. That's ___Ana's___ computer.
   (Ana)

3. That's ___Matt's___ pet.
   (Matt)

4. That's ___Jen's___ pet.
   (Jen)

5. That's ___Ana's___ bike.
   (Ana)

*Possessives, Is there...?/Are there...?* 29

---

## WARMING UP

Show students something they know is yours (your pen, jacket, etc.). Say: *This is my (pen).* Remind students that we use *my* to show that something belongs to us. Go to a student's desk and pick up something that belongs to that student. Say: *This is your (pencil).* Continue with additional examples.

Hold up the Picture Card for *radio* and invite a student to stand with you. Point to you and the student and say: *This is our radio.* Explain that when two or more people own something we say *our.* Continue with additional examples, such as: *This is our classroom. This is our school.* Write examples on the board and read them with students.

Hold up the picture of the house you drew for page 28 and say: *This is my house. This is (Mrs. Star's) house.* Write these sentences on the board and underline the 's. Explain that when something belongs to a person we can show this by writing an apostrophe s at the end of the word. Continue the activity by asking students to tell what belongs to them. Write their names on the board using 's at the end of the word. Read with students, for example: *Tom's pencil, Ana's notebook.*

## USING PAGE 29

Help students find page 29 in their books. Ask them to tell what is happening in each picture. Play the recording or read the Grammar Box with students. Remind students that

we can show possession by adding 's to the end of a person's name.

Read the directions for the activity and ask students to read with you. Ask students to describe each picture. Help students identify and read each person's name. Explain that students will be writing the names using 's to show possession. Read the first sentence. Ask students to trace the word *Taro's.* Then show them how to draw a line from the sentence to the matching picture. Use a similar procedure to complete the page with students. Write the answers on the board and ask students to self-check their work.

## Using Page 30

Help students find page 30 in their books. Read the directions for Exercise A and ask students to follow along. Ask students to tell what they see in the first picture. Help students see that the boy is pointing to himself and that this is his house. Read the sentence: *This is my house.* Ask students to read with you. Ask them to circle the word *my* to complete the sentence. Use a similar procedure to complete the rest of the page. Write the answers on the board so students can self-check their work.

Read the directions for Exercise B and ask students to read with you. Identify each of these items in the picture: *house, window, rug, sink, telephone, radio, door.* As you identify each item, write the words on the board and read them with students. Explain that students should point to each item as they say the corresponding word. Model if necessary.

## Having Fun!
### Whose Is It?

Write the following vocabulary words on the board and read them with students: *house, door, window, telephone, radio, mirror, sink, pet, rug, computer, bike.* Give each student a piece of drawing paper. Ask students to choose a word from the list, draw a picture for their word, and then label it. After you collect the pictures, hold up each one and ask students to guess whose picture it is. Model the first response by saying: *This is Greg's (mirror).* Continue until each student's picture has been identified.

### Information Gap Activity

Make one set of Picture Cards for each student. Ask students to work in pairs. Students sit back-to-back with their Picture Cards. Student 1 holds up a Picture Card. Student 2 guesses

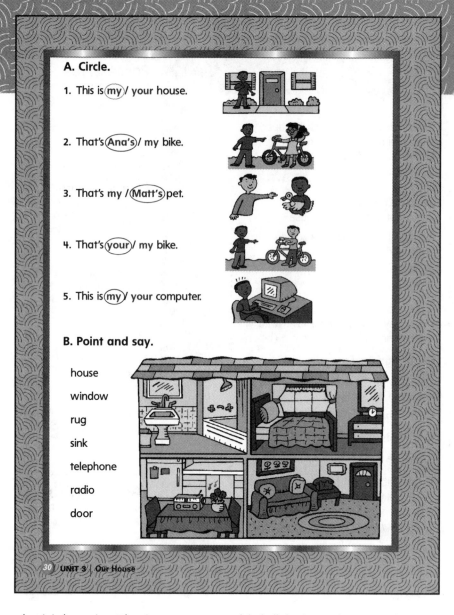

**A. Circle.**

1. This is my / your house.

2. That's Ana's / my bike.

3. That's my / Matt's pet.

4. That's your / my bike.

5. This is my / your computer.

**B. Point and say.**

house
window
rug
sink
telephone
radio
door

what it is by saying: *That is your (pet).* Student 1 answers *yes* or *no.* Student 2 continues to guess until he or she guesses correctly. Students then change roles.

### Draw and Label Your House

Ahead of time, add labels to the picture you have drawn of your house. Label these items: *window, rug, sink, telephone, radio.* Label additional items that students will be familiar with, including family members. Show your picture to students and ask them to tell what they see. Help them read the labels. Give each student a piece of drawing paper and ask them to draw a detailed picture of their houses and family members. Students should also

label all the items they can. When they have finished, invite students to share their work. Students can identify each picture and read their labels.

**Vocabulary:** bike, computer, door, house, mirror, pet, radio, rug, sink, telephone, window

### Lesson Objectives
✓ to identify items in a house

✓ to ask and answer questions with *Is there* and *Are there*

### Classroom English
• Find. Say. Circle. Color. Draw. Write. Show me. What is it?

### Language Patterns
• Is there a (window) in the (house)?

• Are there (windows) in the (house)?

• Yes, there is.

• Yes, there are.

• No, there isn't.

• No, there aren't.

### Materials
• Index cards with the words: *house, door, window, telephone, radio, mirror, sink, pet, rug, computer, bike;* index cards with the plurals for each word; large pieces of poster board; drawing paper, markers, crayons, tape

• **Picture Cards:** house, door, window, telephone, radio, mirror, sink, pet, rug, computer, bike

## WARMING UP

On a large piece of poster board or paper, draw a picture of a house. Include one each of the following items: *door, window, telephone, radio, mirror, sink, rug.* Review each vocabulary word with students and then model the following sentence: *There is a (telephone) in the house.* Ask students to repeat and continue with additional examples.

Now model the question: *Is there a (mirror) in the house?* Ask students to repeat and then model the affirmative short answer: *Yes, there is.* Continue with additional questions and answers that students can practice.

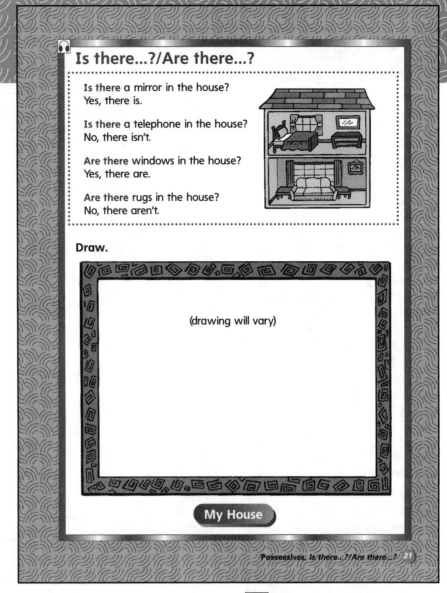

### Is there...?/Are there...?

Is there a mirror in the house?
Yes, there is.

Is there a telephone in the house?
No, there isn't.

Are there windows in the house?
Yes, there are.

Are there rugs in the house?
No, there aren't.

**Draw.**

(drawing will vary)

**My House**

Possessives, *Is there...?/Are there...?* 31

Ask students: *Is there a (pet/computer/bike) in the house?* Ask students to repeat the question after you and then model the negative short answer: *No, there isn't.* Ask students to repeat the responses.

Add additional windows, doors, telephones, radios, sinks, and rugs to your picture. Ask: *Are there (doors) in the house?* Ask students to repeat the question and then model the response: *Yes, there are.* Students repeat.

Now ask: *Are there (pets/computers/bikes) in the house?* Ask students to repeat the question after you. Then model the response: *No, there aren't.* Students repeat.

## USING PAGE 31

Help students find page 31 in their books. Ask them to tell what they see in the picture. Play the recording or read the Grammar Box with students. Remind students that we use *Is there/There is* for questions and answers about one person or thing. We use *Are there/There are* for questions and answers about more than one person or thing.

Explain that students will draw a picture of a house. Ask them to make some singular and some plural. When they are finished, ask students to work in pairs. Students can ask and answer: *Is there a (window) in the house? Are there (computers) in the house?*

## USING PAGE 32

Help students find page 32 in their books. Ask students to tell what they see in the picture. Ask questions and model responses: *Is there a (sink) in the house? Are there (telephones) in the house? Yes, there is. No, there isn't. Yes, there are. No, there aren't.* Read the first question with students. Point to the radio and read the response: *Yes, there is.* Ask students to trace the response. Explain that students will be completing the questions and answers and using the picture as a reference. Complete the page with students and write the answers on the board. When the page is complete, ask students to self-check their work.

## HAVING FUN!
### Information Gap Activity

Give each student a piece of drawing paper and one set of Picture Cards for the vocabulary in this unit. Students draw a picture of a house. Model the activity. Students work in pairs and sit back-to-back. Student 1 chooses five Picture Cards and places them in his or her house. Student 2 asks questions to find out which items are in the house: *Is there a (telephone) in the house?* Student 1 responds either: *Yes, there is.* or *No, there isn't.* Student 2 continues guessing until he or she has guessed all the items in the house, and then looks at Student 1's house to verify his or her answers. Students 1 and 2 change roles and play again.

### Is There?/Are There?

You will need multiple copies of the Picture Cards for this activity. Draw a picture of a house on a large piece of poster board or paper. Place multiple copies of the Picture Cards in a paper bag or box. Invite students to come up, choose a Picture Card, identify it,

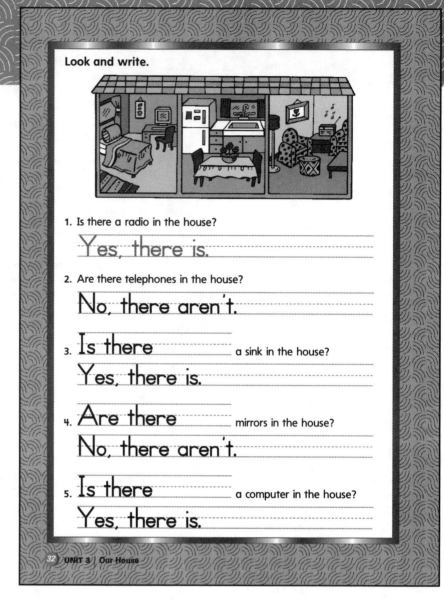

**Look and write.**

1. Is there a radio in the house?

   Yes, there is.

2. Are there telephones in the house?

   No, there aren't.

3. Is there _____ a sink in the house?

   Yes, there is.

4. Are there _____ mirrors in the house?

   No, there aren't.

5. Is there _____ a computer in the house?

   Yes, there is.

and place it in the house by taping it onto the poster board or paper. Continue until each student has had a chance to place one item in the house. Now ask students to take a good look at the picture. Ask questions about their picture: *Is there a (telephone) in the house? Are there (windows) in the house?* Students answer according to the picture they have created. Model affirmative and negative short answers.

### Singular and Plural Matching

Write the following singular nouns on index cards: *house, door, window, telephone, radio, mirror, sink, pet, rug, computer, bike.* Write the plural for each word on an additional set of index cards. Ask students to draw an

outline of a house on drawing paper. Place all the index cards facedown on the table or on the floor in front of students. Model the activity. Students take turns turning over two cards. If they find the singular and plural of a noun, they keep the match and place it in their house. Continue playing until all the matches are found. At the end of the game, students tell what is in their house: *There is a (window) in my house. There are (windows) in my house.*

**Vocabulary:** bike, computer, door, house, mirror, pet, radio, rug, sink, telephone, window

### Lesson Objectives
✓ to identify items in a house

✓ to ask questions with *Is there/Are there*

✓ to offer responses using affirmative and negative short answers *Yes, there is. Yes, there are. No, there isn't. No, there aren't.*

✓ to use the possessives *my, your, our*

### Classroom English
• Show me. Find. Say. This is a (bike). That is a (bike).

### Language Patterns
• Are there (rugs) in the house?

• Is there a (radio) in the house?

• Yes, there is.

• No, there isn't.

• Yes, there are.

• No, there aren't.

### Materials
• Tape

• **Picture Cards:** house, door, window, telephone, radio, mirror, sink, pet, rug, computer, bike

## WARMING UP

Show students Picture Cards to review vocabulary. Ask students to tell what they see. Model if necessary. Draw a picture of a house on the board and tape some of the Picture Cards in the house. Ask: *Is there a (window) in the house?* Ask students to offer responses and model if necessary: *Yes, there is. No, there isn't.* Repeat the activity by placing multiple copies of the Picture Cards in the house. Ask: *Are there (computers) in the house?* Ask students to offer responses: *Yes, there are. No, there aren't.* Model if necessary.

**Chant.**

Are there rugs in the house?
Yes, there are.
Yes, there are.

Are there mirrors in the house?
No, there aren't.
No, there aren't.

Is there a radio in the house?
Yes, there is.
Yes, there is.

Is there a bike in the house?
No, there isn't.
No, there isn't.

Possessives, *Is there...?/Are there...?* 33

##  USING PAGE 33

Help students find page 33 in their books. Play the recording or read the chant aloud. Draw a house on the board with items that correspond to words in the chant. Point to the house and nod or shake your head as appropriate for each stanza. Model and ask students to follow along and point to each word as they listen. After students have listened to and read the chant a few times, invite them to say it with you. Encourage them to point to each word as they read and to act out the actions with you.

## EXTENSION
### Continue the Chant

Review the chant with students by playing the recording or reading it aloud. Substitute other items that are found in the house. Students say the new chant. Invite volunteers to come up and point to the corresponding Picture Cards as they hear them in the chant.

### Take the Parts

Divide the class into two groups. One group asks the question and the second group gives the response. Change roles and repeat.

**Vocabulary:** bike, computer, door, house, mirror, pet, radio, rug, sink, telephone, window

### Lesson Objectives
✓ to identify items in a house

✓ to ask questions with *Is there/Are there*

✓ to offer responses using affirmative and negative short answers *Yes, there is. Yes, there are. No, there isn't. No, there aren't.*

✓ to use the possessives *my, your, our*

✓ to tell what's wrong with a picture

### Classroom English
• Draw. Show me. Find. Say. This is a (bike). That is a (bike).

### Language Patterns
• Are there (rugs) in the house?

• Is there a (radio) in the house?

• Yes, there is.

• No, there isn't.

• Yes, there are.

• No, there aren't.

### Materials
• Crayons, pencils or markers, tape, drawing paper

• **Picture Cards:** house, door, window, telephone, radio, mirror, sink, pet, rug, computer, bike

## WARMING UP

Draw an outline of a house on the board and tape the Picture Cards inside. Ask students to identify each item. Encourage them to use a complete sentence. For example: *It's a computer.* Now take some of the Picture Cards out of the house and tape them next to the house. Ask questions such as: *Is there a (computer) in the house?* Invite students to respond: *Yes, there is.* or *No, there isn't.*

Invite individual students to come up. Give the student a Picture Card and

What's wrong?

ask the class to tell whose it is. For example: *It's (Ana's) (radio).* Then ask the student to tell whose item it is: *It's (my) (house).*

## USING PAGE 34

Help students find page 34 in their books. Ask students to tell what they see in the picture. Help students to tell what is wrong with the picture. Model sentences such as: *There is a (dress) in the (refrigerator).* Ask students to circle all the items that are wrong. When they are finished, ask students to sit with a partner and talk about the picture using vocabulary and language from this unit. Model as necessary.

## EXTENSION
### Draw Your Own Silly Picture

Show students a silly picture you have drawn in advance. Discuss with students what is wrong with your picture. Give each student a piece of drawing paper and ask them to draw a silly picture that is similar to the one on page 34. When they are finished, invite individual students to share their picture with the rest of the class. Encourage them to use vocabulary and language from this unit.

# Unit 4
## My Community

### Prepositions, Adjectives, Proper Nouns

**Vocabulary:** bakery, bank, between, bookstore, hospital, library, on, post office, restaurant, supermarket

### Lesson Objectives
✓ to identify workplaces in the community

✓ to use prepositions to tell the location of places in the community

### Classroom English
• Find. Say. Circle. Color. Draw. Write. Show me. What is this? It is a (hospital). Where is the (hospital)?

### Language Patterns
• It is a (supermarket).

• The (hospital) is (on) Green Street.

• The (bank) is (between) the post office and the restaurant.

### Materials
• Crayons, markers, two sets of Picture Cards

• **Picture Cards:** library, post office, hospital, bank, bakery, bookstore, restaurant, supermarket

## WARMING UP

Show students Picture Cards for *library, post office, hospital, bank, bakery, bookstore, restaurant, supermarket.* Ask students to repeat the words after you say each one. Then use each word in a full sentence. Model and ask students to repeat: *This is a (post office).*

After students are familiar with the new vocabulary, place the Picture Cards facedown in a pile. Model the activity. Students take turns turning over the top card and telling what Picture Card it is. Model if necessary.

Do a Total Physical Response (TPR) activity. Give directions and ask students to place the Picture Cards in the correct places. For example: *Put the hospital between the bank and the bakery.* After students have placed the Picture Cards, ask them to

tell where the middle card is. Model responses if necessary. Write responses on the board and read them with students. Erase the preposition *between* and ask individual students to fill in the missing word.

Draw a street on the board and label it *Green Street.* Place three of the Picture Cards on the street. Model sentences for students to repeat: *The bakery is on Green Street. The post office is on Green Street. The bank is on Green Street.*

After students are familiar with the activity, invite them to follow your directions and to place the Picture Cards on the street. Then ask students to tell where the buildings are: *The bakery is on Green Street.*

Write the responses on the board and read them with students. Erase the preposition *on* and invite individual students to fill in the missing word.

##  USING PAGE 35

Help students find page 35 in their books. Allow students to talk about the pictures and encourage them to use the key vocabulary from this unit. Play the recording or read the words as you point to each place. Ask students to do this with you. Model complete sentences and ask students to repeat as you point to the appropriate Picture Cards: *It is a (post office).*

**Prepositions, Adjectives, Proper Nouns 35**

## USING PAGE 36

Help students find page 36 in their books. Play the recording or read the Grammar Box as you point to the buildings and where they are on the street. Students read with you. Explain that we use the prepositions *between* and *on* to tell the location of places. Explain that *between* means *in the middle.*

Read the directions for the activity and ask students to read with you. Ask students to identify the places in the community and to tell where they are on the streets. Explain that students will complete the sentences with *between* or *on.* Read the first sentence and ask students to find the bank, the bakery, and the restaurant. Ask them to trace the words *bank* and *between.* Use a similar procedure to complete the exercise. Write the answers on the board for students to use as a reference.

## HAVING FUN!
### Three in a Row

Say three vocabulary words and ask students to repeat them after you in the same order in which you said them. Then invite a student to come up, name each one, and place corresponding Picture Cards in the correct order on the board. Ask the student to tell where the middle card is and to use the preposition *between.* Model a response for students: *The bakery is between the post office and the bank.* You can play this game in teams. Divide the class into two teams. Students from each team take turns identifying the cards, placing them in the correct order, and telling where the middle card is. You will need two sets of Picture Cards when students play in teams.

### *The bank is on White Street.*

Draw two streets on the board and label them for students: *White Street* and *Green Street.* Read the street

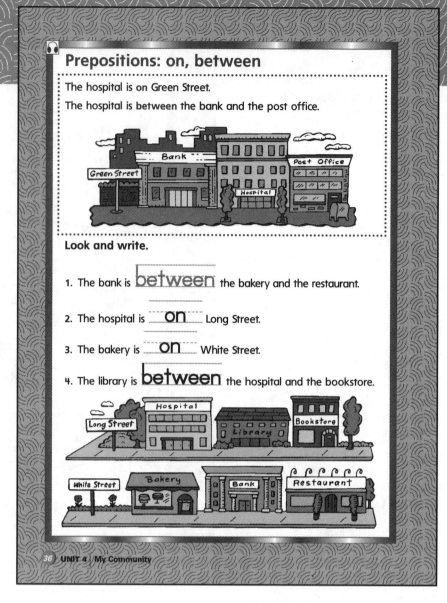

### Prepositions: on, between

The hospital is on Green Street.
The hospital is between the bank and the post office.

**Look and write.**

1. The bank is **between** the bakery and the restaurant.

2. The hospital is ___**on**___ Long Street.

3. The bakery is ___**on**___ White Street.

4. The library is **between** the hospital and the bookstore.

36 UNIT 4 My Community

names with students. Model the activity. Say sentences telling where the buildings are and then invite students to put the appropriate Picture Card on the correct street. For example: *Put the bakery on Green Street.* Ask students to tell where the building is. Model responses if necessary.

After students are familiar with the activity, challenge them to put two buildings on the two different streets. For example: *Put the post office on White Street. Put the bookstore on Green Street.* Ask students to tell where the buildings are. Model responses if necessary.

### Guessing Game

Place the Picture Cards from this unit on the board or on the floor in front

of students. Ask students to identify each Picture Card. Ask students to close their eyes. Take away one Picture Card. Students open their eyes and tell which Picture Card is missing. The student who guesses correctly gets to take away the next Picture Card. As students are playing, encourage them to identify the Picture Cards and to use complete sentences such as: *It is a (post office).*

**Vocabulary:** bakery, bank, between, big, bookstore, hospital, library, new, old, on, post office, restaurant, short, small, supermarket, tall

### Lesson Objectives
✓ to identify workplaces in the community

✓ to use prepositions to tell the location of places in the community

✓ to use adjectives to describe things

### Classroom English
• Find. Say. Circle. Color. Draw. Write. Show me. What is it? It is a (restaurant). Where is the (bakery)?

### Language Patterns
• The (restaurant) is (old).

• The (bank) is (on) (Green Street).

• The (bank) is between the (restaurant) and the (bakery).

### Materials
• Drawing paper; crayons; markers; words on slips of paper: *old, new, big, small, tall, short, restaurant, school, bank, post office, library, bookstore;* one set of Picture Cards for each student; index cards with the words: *library, post office, hospital, bank, bakery, bookstore, restaurant, supermarket;* index cards with the words: *old, new, big, small, tall, short*

• **Picture Cards:** library, post office, hospital, bank, bakery, bookstore, restaurant, supermarket

## WARMING UP

Show students the Picture Cards and review the names of each community workplace. Hold up a Picture Card and ask students to say the vocabulary word with you. Now draw two intersecting streets on the board. Label the streets *Apple Street* and *Long Street.* Say: *The library is on Long Street.* Invite a student to come up, find the *library* Picture Card, and place it on the correct street. Continue with additional examples that allow students to

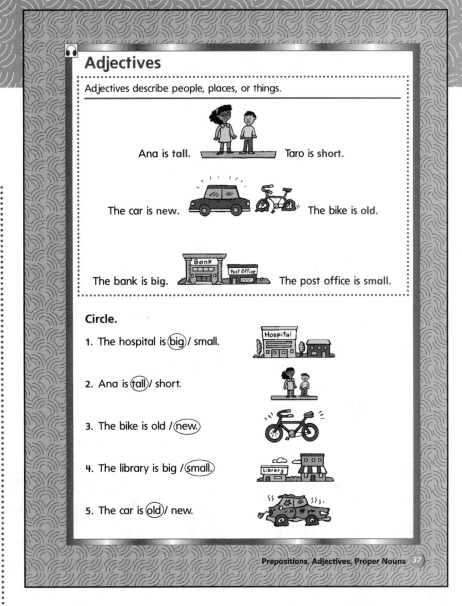

## Adjectives

Adjectives describe people, places, or things.

Ana is tall.    Taro is short.

The car is new.    The bike is old.

The bank is big.    The post office is small.

**Circle.**

1. The hospital is (big) / small.

2. Ana is (tall) / short.

3. The bike is old / (new.)

4. The library is big / (small.)

5. The car is (old) / new.

practice using the preposition *between.*

Draw a picture of a small school and a big hospital on the board. Point to the small school and say: *The school is small.* Ask students to repeat after you. Point to the hospital and say: *The hospital is big.* Ask students to repeat. Repeat the activity, using the adjectives *old, new, tall, short.* Explain that these words are adjectives and that they describe people, places, or things.

## USING PAGE 37

Help students find page 37 in their books. Ask students to talk about the pictures. Play the recording or read the Grammar Box with students.

Explain that these new words are adjectives and are used to describe people, places, or things.

Read the directions for the activity and ask students to read with you. Ask students to identify the pictures and to use an adjective to describe them. Ask students to describe the two buildings in number 1. Read the first sentence with students. Ask them to trace the circle around the word *big* to complete the sentence. Use a similar procedure to complete the page with students.

## USING PAGE 38

Help students find page 38 in their books. Ask students to tell what they see in the top picture. Read the directions for Exercise A and ask students to read with you. Read the first sentence and point to the bank on Apple Street. Next, help students find the bank and the bakery. Read the next sentence and ask students to point to the library between the bank and the bakery. Use a similar procedure to point to the library next to the bakery. Then ask students to say each sentence as they point to the picture.

Read the directions for Exercise B and ask students to read with you. Read the first sentence with students and ask them to tell what they see in the picture. Help students understand that the library is small and that the word *small* best completes this sentence. Use a similar procedure to complete the page with students. Students fill in the missing adjectives. Write the answers on the board so students can self-check their work.

## HAVING FUN!
### Act It Out

Write the following words on slips of paper: *old, new, big, small, tall, short.* Read each word with students and then act each adjective out for them. Fold the slips of paper and place them in a bag or box. Students take turns choosing a slip of paper and acting out the adjective. The student who guesses correctly first gets to act out the next word.

### Make a Sentence

Write the following words on slips of paper: *old, new, big, small, tall, short.* Use the Picture Cards: *library, post office, hospital, bank, bakery, bookstore, restaurant, supermarket.* Place the Picture Cards in a pile.

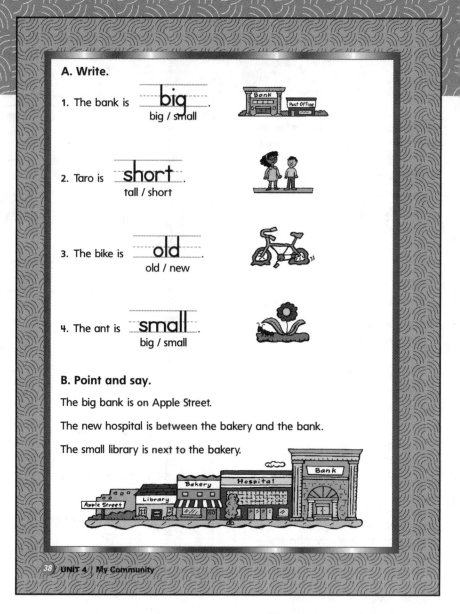

**A. Write.**

1. The bank is ___big___ .
   big / small

2. Taro is ___short___ .
   tall / short

3. The bike is ___old___ .
   old / new

4. The ant is ___small___ .
   big / small

**B. Point and say.**

The big bank is on Apple Street.

The new hospital is between the bakery and the bank.

The small library is next to the bakery.

Model the activity. Students choose a slip of paper and a Picture Card and then say a sentence. For example, if a student chooses *new* and *bakery,* they say: *The bakery is new.*

### Drawing Dictation

Give each student a piece of drawing paper and show them how to fold it into eight boxes. Students draw pictures according to your directions:

*Draw a small restaurant.*
*Draw a big school.*
*Draw a tall bank.*
*Draw a short post office.*
*Draw an old library.*
*Draw a new bookstore.*

When students are finished, do a Show Me activity. Say: *Show me the* big school. Students point to the correct picture and name it.

### Opposites

Write these adjectives on index cards: *old, new, big, small, tall, short.* Make two sets. Read each pair of opposites and help students see the relationship between the words. Place the index cards facedown on a table or on the floor in front of students. Students take turns turning over two index cards. If they find a pair of opposites, they keep the pair. If they do not, they turn over the cards and the game continues. The student with the most pairs at the end of the game wins. Encourage students to use each adjective in a sentence.

**Vocabulary:** bakery, bank, bookstore, hospital, library, post office, restaurant, supermarket

### Lesson Objectives
✓ to identify workplaces in the community
✓ to use prepositions to tell the location of places in the community
✓ to use proper nouns

### Classroom English
• Find. Say. Circle. Color. Draw. Write. Show me. What is it? Where is the (bakery)?

### Language Patterns
• It's a (bakery).
• It's (Tom's) bakery.

### Materials
• Drawing paper; markers; crayons; tape; index cards with the words: *library, post office, hospital, bank, bakery, bookstore, restaurant, supermarket;* index cards with students' names and *'s*
• **Picture Cards:** library, post office, hospital, bank, bakery, bookstore, restaurant, supermarket

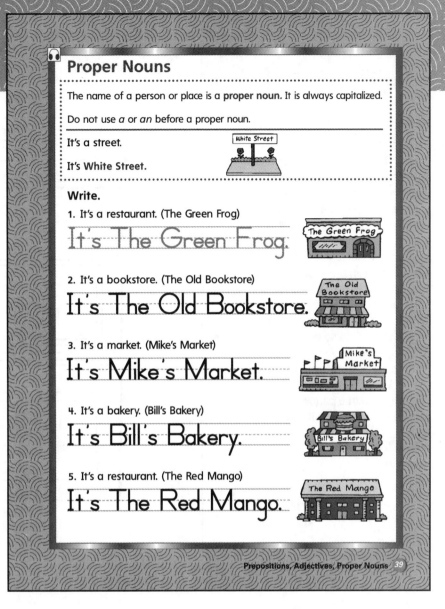

### WARMING UP

Show students the Picture Cards for this unit and ask them to identify each building. Pick up one Picture Card and say: *It's a (bakery).* Ask students to repeat. Invite a student to come up. Hand him or her a Picture Card and model the sentence: *It's (Bob's) Bakery.* Write both sentences on the board and read them with students. Explain that *bakery* describes the <u>kind</u> of place. Explain that *Bob's Bakery* is a proper noun that tells the name of a specific place. All proper nouns start with a capital letter. Explain that we don't use *a* or *an* before a proper noun. Continue the activity by inviting other students to come up. Allow them to choose a Picture Card. The rest of the class tells whose building it is, using the

language modeled in this lesson. Write the sentences on the board and read them with students.

### 🎧 USING PAGE 39

Help students find page 39 in their books. Play the recording or read the Grammar Box with students. Explain that the name of a person or place is a proper noun and is always capitalized.

Read the directions for the writing activity and ask students to read with you. Ask students to look at the pictures. Help them identify the proper nouns. Read the first sentence in number 1 with students and then point to the picture. Read the second sentence and help students see that

it was rewritten using a proper noun. Ask students to trace the sentence. Remind students that we do not use *a* or *an* before a proper noun. Use a similar procedure to complete the page with students. Write the new sentences on the board and ask students to self-check their work.

## USING PAGE 40

Help students find page 40 in their books. Read the directions for the activity. Ask students to tell what they see in the picture: *door, window.* Draw a sample picture of a restaurant on the board and ask students to tell what they see. Include places for a sign to name the restaurant, and windows where they can draw food or people eating. Draw at least two different possibilities as models. You may want students to include a street sign, a tree, a street, and so on for additional language practice. Ask students to finish drawing the restaurants in their books. When they are finished, ask them to sit with a partner and to compare and contrast their pictures.

## HAVING FUN!
### Riddles

Place the Picture Cards for this unit on the board. Say the following riddles for students:

*I eat here.*
*I find books here.*
*I buy books here.*
*I mail a letter here.*
*I see a doctor here.*
*I put my money here.*
*I buy food here.*
*I find cake here.*

Students guess which community workplace you are talking about and take the corresponding Picture Card. The student with the most Picture Cards at the end of the game wins.

### Which one is it?

Draw two intersecting streets on the board. Label the streets *White Street* and *Green Street.* Tape the Picture Cards on the streets. Say sentences that give clues about one of the buildings. For example: *It's on White Street. It's between the bank and the library. What is it?* After students have solved a few riddles like this, invite them to make riddles for their

**Draw and color.**

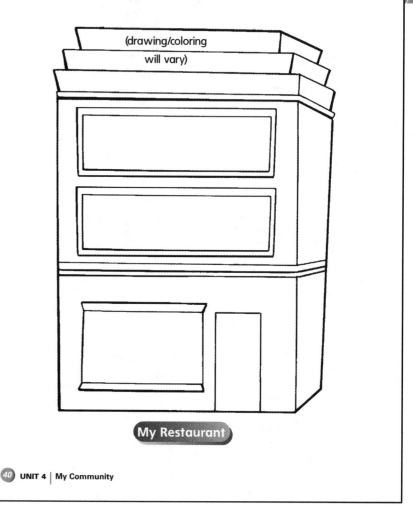

(drawing/coloring will vary)

My Restaurant

40 UNIT 4 | My Community

classmates. The student to guess correctly first gets to ask the next riddle.

### Go to the bakery.

Place the Picture Cards for this unit around the classroom. Point out where each building Picture Card is and invite students to identify which one it is. Then give Total Physical Response (TPR) commands such as: *Go to the (bakery).* When students get to a place, ask them to identify the building.

### Whose (bakery) is it?

Ahead of time, write students' names on index cards. Include *'s* at the end of each students' name. Read the cards with students. Place the Picture Cards in a pile facedown on the table.

Place the index cards in a second pile, facedown on the table. Model the activity. Students take turns choosing a Picture Card and a name card. Then they say a sentence using a proper noun: *It's Alex's (library).* Model responses if necessary.

**Vocabulary:** bakery, bank, bookstore, hospital, library, new, post office, restaurant, small, supermarket, tall

### Lesson Objectives
✓ to identify community workplaces
✓ to use prepositions to tell the location of places in the community
✓ to use adjectives to describe things
✓ to use proper nouns

### Classroom English
• Draw. Show me. Find. Say. It's a (bakery). It's (Bob's) bakery. The bakery is (small).

### Language Patterns
• It is a (supermarket).
• The (hospital) is on Green Street.
• The (bank) is (between) the (post office) and the (bookstore).

### Materials
• Crayons and pencils or markers, drawing paper, tape
• **Picture Cards:** library, post office, hospital, bank, bakery, bookstore, restaurant, supermarket

🎧 **Chant.**

The bakery is new.
It's Tom's Bakery.
It's Tom's Bakery.

The restaurant is small.
It's Jo's Restaurant.
It's Jo's Restaurant.

The bookstore is tall.
It's Sam's Bookstore.
It's Sam's Bookstore.

Prepositions, Adjectives, Proper Nouns  41

## WARMING UP

Review vocabulary from this unit. Show students the Picture Cards and ask them to tell what they see. Place three Picture Cards on the board and ask students to identify the one that is between the others. Encourage them to use the preposition *between*. Model examples if necessary. Draw a picture of a street on the board and place two or three Picture Cards on the street. Ask students to tell where they are: *The (bank) is on (White Street).*

 **USING PAGE 41**

Help students find page 41 in their books. Play the recording or read the chant aloud. Model and ask students to follow along and point to each word as they listen. After they have

listened to and read the chant a few times, invite students to say it with you. Encourage them to point to each word as they read. Place the corresponding Picture Cards on the board. Say the chant again and invite students to come up and point to the corresponding Picture Cards as they hear them in the chant.

## EXTENSION
### Continue the Chant

Review the chant with students by playing the recording or reading it for them. Substitute other community workplaces and names. You can also use students' names for this part of the activity. Students say the new chant. Invite volunteers to come up

and point to the corresponding Picture Cards as they hear them in the chant. Students can also point to the student who is named.

### Take the Parts

Divide the class into two groups. One group can read the first sentence for each verse. The second group can read the last two sentences for each verse. Reverse roles and repeat.

**Vocabulary:** bakery, bank, between, bookstore, hospital, in, library, next to, on, post office, restaurant, supermarket

Find me!

Park

Bookstore

School

Supermarket

Restaurant

Bank

Pets

Shoes

Library

42 UNIT 4 | My Community

## WARMING UP

Draw two streets on the board and tape Picture Cards on each street. Ask students to identify the community workplaces, and tell where they are. For example: *It is a (supermarket). The (supermarket) is (between) the (bookstore) and the (post office).* Model if necessary.

Draw simple pictures on the board that use the vocabulary from this unit including the adjectives: *big, small, old, new, tall, short.* Ask students to identify each community workplace and then to describe it. For example: *It is a (post office). The (post office) is (small).* Model if necessary.

## USING PAGE 42

Help students find page 42 in their books. Ask students to tell what they

see. Then ask them to find the buildings and to tell where they are. Model sentences such as: *The bank is next to the supermarket.* Then ask students to find the ducks and to tell where they are. Students can use the prepositions *in, on, between,* and *next to* when responding.

## EXTENSION
### Where is it in your town?

Show students a picture of a town you have drawn in advance. Ask students to tell what they see and to tell where the buildings and people are. Give each student a piece of drawing paper and ask them to draw a picture similar to the one on page 42. When they are finished, invite students to work with a partner. Students switch drawings and

find the buildings, people, and other items drawn.

### Partner Art

Have students draw simple pictures of a town with buildings and streets. Do not let them see each other's drawings. Then give extra drawing paper to each student. Place students in pairs, back-to-back. One student begins giving instructions so that his or her partner can duplicate his or her drawing without seeing it. For example: *Draw a bank. Draw a library next to the bank.* Students exchange roles, and the second student then gives instructions for his or her drawing to be duplicated. Students compare how similar their drawings are after they finish.

# Units 3 & 4
**Review**

**Vocabulary:** bakery, bank, bike, bookstore, computer, door, hospital, house, library, mirror, pet, post office, radio, restaurant, rug, sink, supermarket, telephone, window

### Review Objectives
✓ to identify items in a house
✓ to identify prepositions of place
✓ to identify workplaces in the community
✓ to identify questions with *Is there* and *Are there*
✓ to identify short answers with *There is* and *There are*

### Classroom English
• Listen. Check. Color. Point. Say.

### Language Patterns
• The (bank) is on (Green Street).
• The (bank) is (between) the (bakery) and the (library).
• The (bike) is new.
• Is there (a rug) in the room?
• Yes, there is.
• No, there isn't.
• Are there (windows) in the house?
• Yes, there are.
• No, there aren't.

### Materials
• **Picture Cards:** house, door, window, telephone, radio, mirror, sink, pet, rug, computer, bike, library, post office, hospital, bank, bakery, bookstore, restaurant, supermarket

## WARMING UP

Use Picture Cards to review the vocabulary words from Units 3 and 4. Ask: *What is it?* Invite students to use a complete sentence when

---

## Review: Units 3 and 4

### Vocabulary
**A. Listen and check.**

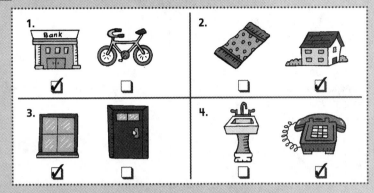

### Prepositions
**B. Listen and check.**

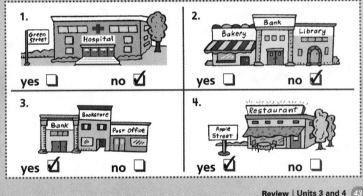

Review | Units 3 and 4 43

---

answering: *It's a (bank).*

Draw two streets on the board and label one *Green Street.* Label the other street *West Street.* Identify the streets with students. Tape Picture Cards such as the *bank, hospital, bakery, restaurant,* or *supermarket* on the street so that some are between other buildings. Ask students to tell where the buildings are. Model sentences such as: *The (bakery) is on (West Street).*

Draw simple pictures on the board to illustrate the following: *The (bakery) is (small, big, old, new, tall, short).* Ask students to identify the buildings and then to use an adjective to describe them. Model sentences and then ask students to say sentences of their own.

Tape two different Picture Cards to the board and draw a small box under each one. Say (*It's/It is) a (hospital).* Point to each Picture Card and ask students to tell you which card matches your sentence. Invite a

---

student to place a check in the correct box.

On the board, tape the (*bakery*) Picture Card next to the (*post office*) Picture Card. Write *yes* and *no* under the Picture Cards and draw a small box next to each of the words *yes* and *no*. Say: *The bakery is behind the post office.* Students should verify if the sentence you said is correct or incorrect according to the picture. Show students how to check the *no* box.

If you feel students need to practice exercises that are similar to those presented in the Review Units, use exercises like the two previous ones so students can practice checking boxes and pictures that go with stated sentences and words. You can use similar exercises for any of the Review Exercises at the end of the unit.

## USING PAGE 43

Help students find page 43 in their books. Help students find Exercise A. Read the directions and ask students to follow along. Point to each picture and ask students to say the words with you. Explain to students that they should check the picture that goes with the word they hear. Play the recording or read the audioscript. Students check the correct picture.

Help students find Exercise B. Read the directions and ask students to follow along. Point to the picture and ask students to tell you where each building is. Explain to students that they should check the *yes* box if the picture goes with the sentence they hear. They should check the *no* box if the picture does not go with the

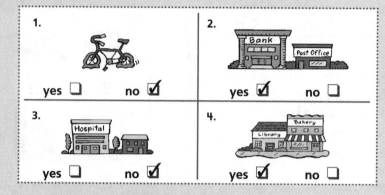

sentence they hear. Play the recording or read the audioscript. Students check the correct picture.

## USING PAGE 44

Help students find page 44 in their books. Help students find Exercise C. Read the directions and ask students to follow along. Point to the pictures and ask students to describe each item. Explain to students that they should check the *yes* box if the

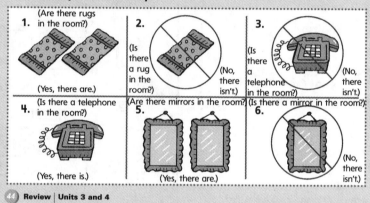

picture goes with the sentence they hear. They should check the *no* box if the picture does not go with the sentence they hear. Play the recording or read the audioscript. Students check the correct picture.

Help students find Exercise D. Read the directions and ask students to follow along. Explain that they should listen, find, and point to the corresponding picture, and then say the question and answer. Play the recording or read the audioscript.

---

### AUDIOSCRIPT

**C.** 1. The bike is new.  2. The bank is tall.  3. The hospital is small.  4. The library is small.

**D.** 1. Are there rugs in the room? Yes, there are.  2. Is there a rug in the room? No, there isn't.
3. Is there a telephone in the room? No, there isn't.  4. Is there a telephone in the room? Yes, there is.
5. Are there mirrors in the room? Yes, there are.  6. Is there a mirror in the room? No, there isn't.

# Unit 5
**Workers**

**Vocabulary:** clerk, cook, dentist, doctor, firefighter, librarian, mail carrier, nurse, police officer, teacher, vet (veterinarian)

**Lesson Objectives**
✓ to identify community helpers
✓ to say and write questions with *what*

**Classroom English**
• Find. Say. Circle. Color. Draw. Write. Show me.

**Language Patterns**
• What does (she) do?
• (She's) a (dentist).

**Materials**
• Crayons; markers; drawing paper; slips of paper with: *doctor, nurse, police officer, firefighter, cook, dentist, vet, mail carrier, librarian, teacher, clerk;* one Bingo grid for each student; Bingo markers; box or bag
• **Picture Cards:** doctor, nurse, police officer, firefighter, cook, dentist, vet, mail carrier, teacher, clerk

## WARMING UP

Show students the following Picture Cards: *doctor, nurse, police officer, firefighter, cook, dentist, vet, mail carrier, librarian, teacher, clerk.* Introduce one word at a time. Ask students to repeat the words after you. Then use each word in a full sentence. Model and ask students to repeat: *(She) is a (dentist).*

Hold up one of the Picture Cards and model the question: *What does (he) do?* Ask students to say it with you. Model the response and ask students to repeat: *(He's a teacher.)* Repeat the activity, having students practice asking and answering the question, using all the Picture Cards.

 ## USING PAGE 45

Help students find page 45 in their books. Play the recording or read the words as you point to each one.

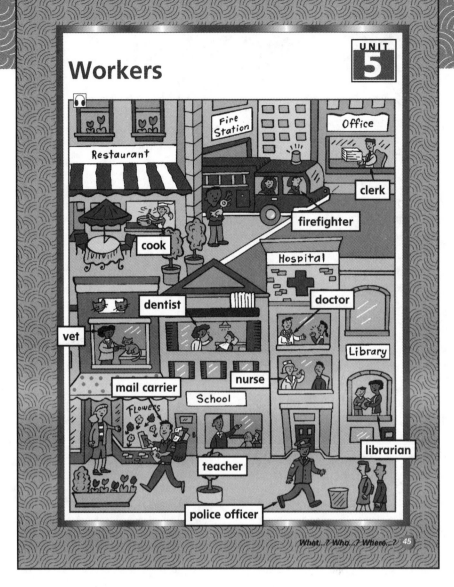

Allow students to talk about the pictures and encourage them to use key vocabulary from this unit. As you say each word, point to the pictures. Ask students to do this with you. Model complete sentences and ask students to repeat as you point to the Picture Cards: *(He) is a (teacher).*

Ask students to listen and follow the directions:

*Draw a blue circle around the doctor.*
*Draw a purple circle around the nurse.*
*Draw a red circle around the police officer.*
*Draw an orange circle around the firefighter.*
*Draw a yellow circle around the cook.*
*Draw a green circle around the dentist.*
*Draw a blue circle around the vet.*

*Draw a purple circle around the mail carrier.*
*Draw a brown circle around the librarian.*
*Draw a red circle around the teacher.*
*Draw a blue circle around the clerk.*

## 🎧 USING PAGE 46

Help students find page 46 in their books. Play the recording or read the Grammar Box as you point to the community helpers. Explain that when we want to ask what a person does for a living we can use the question: *What does (he/she) do?* The response tells what job the person has.

Read the directions for the activity and ask students to read with you. Ask students to identify each community helper. Read the question and response for number 1. Ask students to write the question by tracing the words.

Read the response for number 2. Help students write the question on the line. Write the question on the board for students to use as a reference. Use a similar procedure to complete the page. Ask students to self-check their work.

## HAVING FUN!

### Act It Out

Write the community workers' names on slips of paper. Read each one with students and then place them in a bag or box. Model the activity. Students take turns choosing a slip of paper and acting out what the community helper does. As students are acting, ask: *What does (he) do?* The student who first guesses correctly becomes the next actor.

### Community Helper Bingo

Prepare Bingo grids with nine spaces for each student. Use paper clips or small pieces of paper for markers. Give each student a grid. Write the community helper names on the board and read them with students. Ask students to write the name of one worker in each box and to draw a simple picture for each name. Tell

students that everyone's Bingo grid should be different. One space should be labeled *Free*. Call out worker names randomly. Students place markers on the pictures. Three in a row wins. The winner says a sentence for each word in the winning row: *He's a (cook).*

### Draw Your Favorite Community Helper

Show students a picture you have drawn of your favorite community helper. Ask them to tell who it is. Ask: *What does (she) do?* Encourage students to answer: *(She) is a (librarian).* Give each student a piece of drawing paper. Ask them to draw their favorite community helper.

When they are finished, ask students to share their work with a partner. Then, have students circulate among their classmates. Students ask and answer: *What does (he) do? (He's) a (mail carrier).*

**Vocabulary:** clerk, cook, dentist, doctor, firefighter, librarian, mail carrier, nurse, police officer, teacher, vet

**Lesson Objectives**
✓ to identify community helpers
✓ to say and write questions with *what* and *who*

**Classroom English**
• Find. Say. Circle. Color. Draw. Write. Show me.

**Language Patterns**
• What does (he) do?
• (He's) a (vet).
• Who is (she)?
• (She's) (Dr. Brown).

**Materials**
• Bag or box, large piece of poster board, old magazines, Picture Cards from Unit 4: *hospital, restaurant, post office, school, library, bank*
• **Picture Cards:** doctor, nurse, police officer, firefighter, cook, dentist, vet, mail carrier, librarian, teacher, clerk

## WARMING UP

Show students the Picture Cards from this Unit and review the names of each community worker. Hold up a Picture Card and ask students to say the vocabulary word with you. Ask: *What does (he) do?* Ask students to repeat the response: *(He's) a (firefighter).* Continue in this manner, having students practice asking and answering the question for each community helper. Write the questions and answers on the board and read them with students.

Invite a student to come up. Ask the class: *Who is (she)?* Model the response: *She's (Anna).* Continue the activity, asking other students to participate. Write the questions: *Who is he? Who is she?* on the board and read them with students. Underline the question word *who* and explain

### Who ...?

Who is he?
He's Mr. Black.
He's a firefighter.

Who is she?
She's Dr. White.
She's a dentist.

**Write.**

1.
Who is she?
She's Dr. Brown.
She's a vet.

2.
Who is he?
He's Mr. Long.
He's a mail carrier.

3.
Who is she?
She's Mrs. Small.
She's a librarian.

*What...? Who...? Where...?* 47

that we use this question word when we ask about a person. Explain that when we ask: *Who is (he)?* the response usually contains the person's name. Show students the Picture Cards for *vet, mail carrier,* and *librarian.* Model the question and answer for each community helper and ask students to repeat: *Who is she? She's Dr. Brown. Who is he? He's Mr. Long. Who is she? She's Mrs. Small.* Write the questions and answers on the board and read them with students. Now ask about each community helper: *What does (he) do?* Elicit responses. Write the answers under the corresponding question: *She's a vet. He's a mail carrier. She's a librarian.* Read the sentences with students.

 **USING PAGE 47**

Help students find page 47 in their books. Ask students to tell who they see in the pictures. Play the recording or read the Grammar Box with students. Remind students that we use the question word *who* when we ask about people.

Read the directions for the activity and ask students to read with you. Ask students to identify the community helpers. Read the question and responses in number 1. Ask students to trace the question and second response. Students write the questions and responses. Complete the page with students. Write the answers on the board so students can self-check their work.

## Using Page 48

Help students find page 48 in their books. Read the directions for the activity and ask students to read with you. Ask students to tell who they see in the pictures. Read the question and answer in number 1 and ask them to read with you. Ask students to trace the words to complete the sentences. Show them how to draw a line from the question to the matching picture. Students complete the questions and responses and match them to the correct pictures. Complete the page with students.

## Having Fun!
### A Listening Game

Place the Picture Cards on the board and identify the community helpers with students. Ask students to form a line from the front to the back of the room. Whisper the name of one of the community helpers to the first student in line. Motion for him or her to whisper it to the next student in line. Students continue whispering until the last student is reached. The last student says the name of the community helper and finds the matching Picture Card. As students are playing, change their places in line so that each gets to be either the first or last student. You may want to form more than one line so that more students can participate at one time.

## Community Helpers Mural

Ahead of time, prepare a mural of community helpers. Show students the finished mural and explain that they will be making similar murals. Divide the class into groups. Give each group a large piece of poster board and old magazines. If these are not available, students can draw pictures. As students work, encourage them to use the language from this unit.

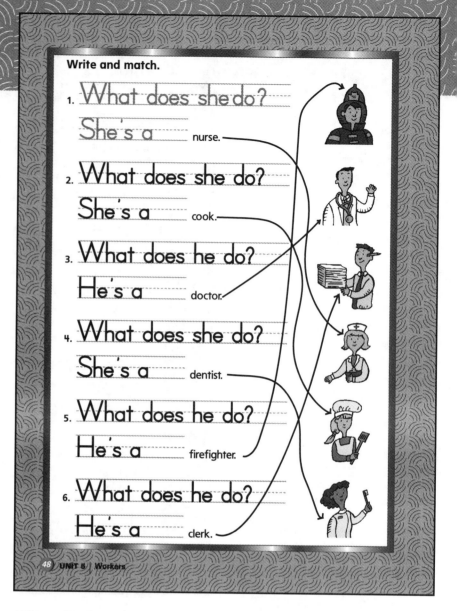

Write and match.

1. What does she do?
   She's a _____ nurse.

2. What does she do?
   She's a _____ cook.

3. What does he do?
   He's a _____ doctor.

4. What does she do?
   She's a _____ dentist.

5. What does he do?
   He's a _____ firefighter.

6. What does he do?
   He's a _____ clerk.

48 UNIT 5 | Workers

## Who and What Sorting

Use these Picture Cards from Unit 4: *hospital, restaurant, post office, school, library, bank.* Ask students to identify the community workplaces. Now show students the following Picture Cards from this unit: *nurse, doctor, cook, mail carrier, teacher, librarian, clerk.* Ask students to identify each community helper. Place two bags or boxes on a table or on the floor in front of students. Label one: *Who.* Label the other one: *What.* Model a question and response for one of the community helpers: *Who is (he)? (He's) a (dentist).* Ask students to repeat. Model a question and response for one of the community workplaces: *What is this? This is a (hospital).* Students take turns sorting the Picture Cards into the correct bags or boxes. As they are sorting, ask students to say the question and answer.

## Information Gap Activity

Students work in pairs. Give each pair one set of Picture Cards. Show them how to sort them into two piles, one for *he* and one for *she.* Model the activity. One student takes the *he* pile and the other student takes the *she* pile. Ask students to sit back-to-back. Student 1 chooses one of the Picture Cards and asks: *What does (she) do?* Student 2 guesses who it is by saying: *She's a (vet).* Student 2 continues guessing until he or she guesses correctly. Students then switch roles and play again.

**Vocabulary:** clerk, cook, dentist, doctor, firefighter, librarian, mail carrier, nurse, police officer, teacher, vet

**Lesson Objectives**

✓ to identify community helpers

✓ to say and write questions with *where*

**Classroom English**

• Find. Say. Circle. Color. Draw. Write. Show me. What is it? Who is it?

**Language Patterns**

• Where does a (doctor) work?

• A (doctor) works in a (hospital).

**Materials**

• Picture Cards from Unit 4: *library, post office, hospital, bank, restaurant;* one set of Picture Cards for each student

• **Picture Cards:** doctor, nurse, police officer, firefighter, cook, dentist, vet, mail carrier, librarian, teacher, clerk

## WARMING UP

Show students the following Picture Cards from this unit: *nurse, doctor, teacher, cook, mail carrier, librarian.* Ask: *Who is (he)?* Elicit responses from students and model if necessary: *(He's) a (teacher).* Now show students these Picture Cards from Unit 4: *hospital, school, restaurant, library, post office.* Ask: *What is this?* Elicit responses and model if necessary: *It's a (library).* Now help students match the community helper to the community workplace. Then, ask: *Where does a (doctor) work?* Ask students to repeat. Model the response and ask students to say it with you: *A (doctor) works in a (hospital).* Continue the activity, having students practice asking and answering questions with *where.* Write the questions and responses on the board and read them with students.

## USING PAGE 49

Help students find page 49 in their books. Ask students to identify the

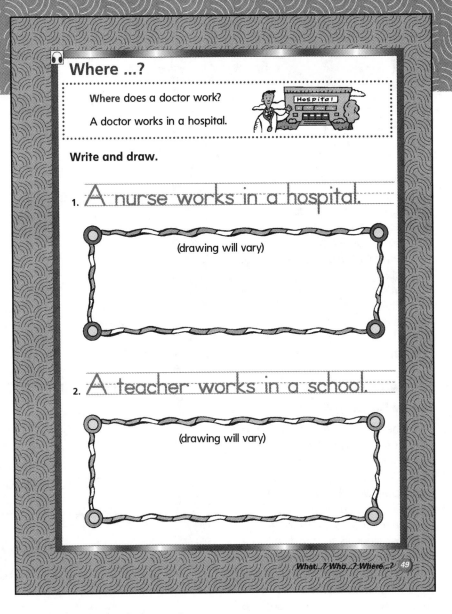

### Where ...?

Where does a doctor work?

A doctor works in a hospital.

**Write and draw.**

1. A nurse works in a hospital.

(drawing will vary)

2. A teacher works in a school.

(drawing will vary)

community helper and community workplace. Play the recording or read the Grammar Box with students. Explain that we use the question word *where* when we want to know the location of someone or something.

Explain to students that they will trace a sentence and then illustrate that sentence by drawing a picture in the box provided. Invite students to tell you what items they will include in their drawing for each sentence. When students have finished their drawings, invite them to show their work to the class.

## USING PAGE 50

Help students find page 50 in their books. Ask students to tell who and what they see in the pictures. Read the first question with the class and explain that the word *nurse* best completes the question. Students trace the word *nurse.* Read the response and explain that the words *nurse* and *hospital* best complete the response. Students trace the words *nurse* and *hospital.* Students complete the questions and answers about each picture. Write the answers on the board so students can self-check their work.

## HAVING FUN
### Where Do They Work?

Place the following Picture Cards from Unit 4 on the board: *library, post office, hospital, bank, restaurant.* Help students identify the community workplaces. Model if necessary. Use these Picture Cards from Unit 5: *librarian, mail carrier, doctor, clerk, cook.* Ask students to identify the community helpers. Model the activity. Students match the worker to the workplace. Ask: *Where does a (doctor) work?* Encourage students to answer: *A (doctor) works in a (hospital).* Model if necessary.

Now place all the Picture Cards facedown on a table or floor in front of students. Students take turns turning over two Picture Cards. If they match the worker to the workplace, they keep the pair. The student with the most pairs at the end of the game wins. Encourage students to use the questions and answers from this lesson as they are playing. You may want to use several sets of cards so that more students can participate at one time.

### Guessing Game

Place the following Picture Cards from this unit on the board: *doctor, nurse, police officer, firefighter, cook, dentist,*

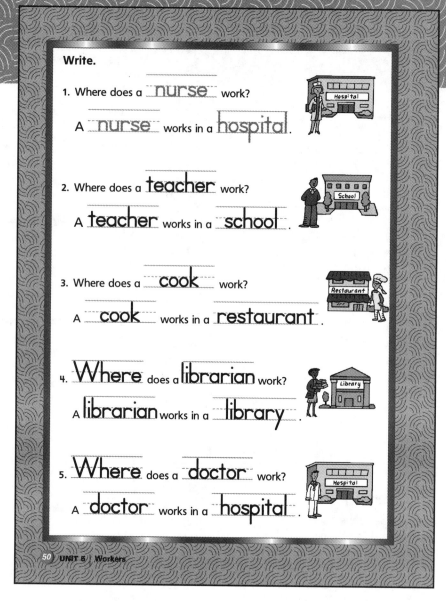

vet, mail carrier, librarian, teacher, clerk. Place these Picture Cards from Unit 4 on the board: *hospital, restaurant, post office, library, school, bank.* Ask students to identify the pictures. Ask: *Who is (he)? What is this?* Ask students to close their eyes and take away one of the Picture Cards. Ask students to open their eyes. Ask: *Who is it?* or *What is it?* Students guess which card is missing by saying: *He is a (teacher).* or *It is a (bank).* The student who guesses correctly first gets to take away the next card and ask the question. Model if necessary.

### Matching Race

You will need one set of each of the following Picture Cards from Unit 4 for each student: *hospital, restaurant,*

post office, library, school, bank. You will also need these Picture Cards from Unit 5: *nurse, cook, mail carrier, librarian, teacher, clerk.* Students work in pairs. Students race to match the community helper to the community workplace. To win a point for each picture, students must also say: *A (doctor) works in a (hospital).* The student with the most points at the end of the game wins.

**Vocabulary:** clerk, cook, dentist, doctor, firefighter, librarian, mail carrier, nurse, police officer, teacher, vet

**Lesson Objectives**

✓ to identify community helpers

✓ to ask questions with *who, what,* and *where*

**Classroom English**

• Play. Show me. Find. Say. It's a (bank). (He's) a (dentist).

**Language Patterns**

• Who is (he)?

• He's a (nurse).

• Where does a (doctor) work?

• A (doctor) works in a (hospital).

• What does (he) do?

• He's a (clerk).

**Materials**

• **Picture Cards:** doctor, nurse, police officer, firefighter, cook, dentist, vet, mail carrier, librarian, teacher, clerk

## WARMING UP

Review vocabulary and language patterns from this unit. Show students the Picture Cards and ask them to tell what they see. Use the language patterns from this unit to ask questions. Model if necessary. Say the names of three community helpers. Students then say the names of the community helpers and place the Picture Cards in the order in which you said them.

 ## USING PAGE 51

Help students find page 51 in their books. Play the recording or read the chant for students. Point to each picture as the word appears in the chant. Model and ask students to follow along and point to each word as they listen. After they have listened to and read the chant a few times, invite students to say it with you. Encourage students to point to each

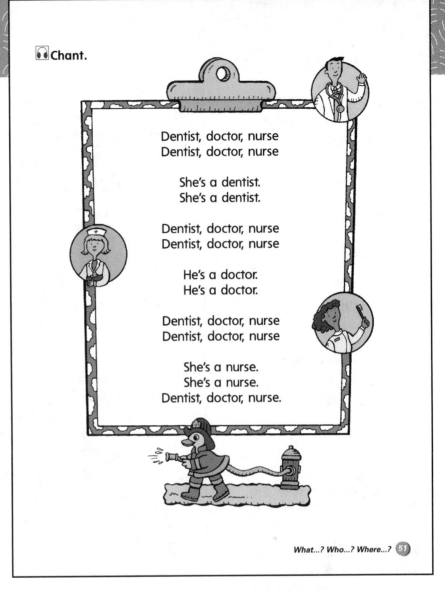

Chant.

Dentist, doctor, nurse
Dentist, doctor, nurse

She's a dentist.
She's a dentist.

Dentist, doctor, nurse
Dentist, doctor, nurse

He's a doctor.
He's a doctor.

Dentist, doctor, nurse
Dentist, doctor, nurse

She's a nurse.
She's a nurse.
Dentist, doctor, nurse.

*What...? Who...? Where...?* 51

word as they read. Place the corresponding Picture Cards on the board. Say the chant again and invite students to come up and point to the corresponding Picture Cards as they hear them in the chant.

## EXTENSION
### Continue the Chant

Review the chant with students by playing the recording or reading it for them. Substitute other community helpers. Students say the new chant. Invite volunteers to come up and point to the corresponding Picture Cards as they hear the community helpers in the chant. Students can also act out what each community helper does.

### Take the Parts

Divide the class into two groups. Group 1 says the first, third, and fifth stanzas. Group 2 says the second, fourth, and sixth stanzas. Groups alternate saying each part and then switch roles.

**Vocabulary:** clerk, cook, dentist, doctor, firefighter, librarian, mail carrier, nurse, police officer, teacher, vet

### Lesson Objectives
✓ to identify community helpers
✓ to ask questions with *who, what,* and *where*

### Classroom English
• Play. Show me. Find. Say. It's a (bank). (He's) a (dentist).

### Language Patterns
• Who is (he)?
• He's a (nurse).
• Where does a (doctor) work?
• A (doctor) works in a (hospital).
• What does (he) do?
• He's a (clerk).

### Materials
• Index cards, tape
• **Picture Cards:** doctor, nurse, police officer, firefighter, cook, dentist, vet, mail carrier, librarian, teacher, clerk

## WARMING UP

Review vocabulary from this unit. Show students the Picture Cards and ask them to identify each community helper. Now tape the Picture Cards on the board in a circle or a square to create a game board. Label the start and finish. Write the numerals *0, 1,* and *2* on index cards three times so there are nine cards. Shuffle the cards and place them facedown in a pile. Invite students to come up, turn over the top card, and move along the game board. Encourage students to name each community helper as they move. Students can use a complete sentence: *(He's) a (dentist).* The game is over when the last Picture Card is reached. You can also ask students to tell where each community helper works: *Where does a (doctor) work?* Encourage them to answer using a complete

What ...? Who ...? Where ...?

sentence: *A (doctor) works in a (hospital).* Model if necessary.

## USING PAGE 52

Help students find page 52 in their books and show them the game board. Ask students to tell who they see. Model how the game is played. Students play in groups of three or four. Write the question words on index cards for each group: *Who? What? Where?* Students place the index cards at the top of their board games. Write the numerals *1* and *2* (three times each) on index cards, so students have six numeral cards to choose from. Students shuffle these cards and place them facedown in the middle of the table. Use paper clips or small colored pieces of paper

as markers. The first student picks a numeral card and moves his or her game piece ahead. Then he or she chooses a question word and asks the question: *Where does a (nurse) work?* He or she then supplies the answer: *A (nurse) works in a (hospital).* Students will not have the vocabulary to ask *where* questions for all of the community helpers. Encourage them to choose a different question word or provide the additional vocabulary needed.

## EXTENSION

Students can play a simpler version of the game by moving their marker along the game board and naming what is on each space. The student who reaches the finish line first wins.

# Unit 6
## My Day

### Simple Present, *When...?*

**Vocabulary:** eat breakfast, eat dinner, eat lunch, get dressed, go home, go to school, go to sleep, listen to music, play the piano, wake up

**Lesson Objectives**
✓ to identify daily activities
✓ to tell time to the hour, quarter hour, and half hour
✓ to use the simple present tense with *I*

**Classroom English**
• Find. Say. Circle. Color. Draw. Write. Show me. What do you do? What time is it? What is it? It's (lunch).

**Language Patterns**
• I (wake up) at (6:00).
• I (go to school).
• It's (lunch).

**Materials**
• Crayons, markers, drawing paper, scissors, paper plates, brads or butterfly clips, one set of Picture Cards for each student, template for hour and minute hands for clocks
• **Picture Cards:** wake up, go to sleep, go to school, eat breakfast, eat lunch, eat dinner, get dressed, listen to music, play the piano, go home

## My Day

| | | |
|---|---|---|
| wake up | eat breakfast | get dressed |
| go to school | eat lunch | go home |
| play the piano | eat dinner | listen to music |
| go to sleep | | |

Simple Present, *When...?* 53

### WARMING UP

Show students the Picture Cards and introduce one verb at a time. Ask students to repeat the verbs after you say each one. Then use each word in a full sentence. Model and ask students to repeat: *I (go to school).*

Use a clock suitable for teaching or make one from a paper plate. Write numerals and cut out an hour hand and a minute hand. Fasten them to the clock with a brad so the hands on the clock move.

Point and count from one to twelve with students, asking: *What number is this?* Go around the clock, having students repeat each hour after you: *It's one o'clock. It's two o'clock.*

Say sentences, such as: *It's seven o'clock. It's time to wake up.* After thorough practice, say: *It's time to wake up. What time is it?* as you point to the numeral 7. Elicit from students: *It's seven o'clock.*

If students know the numbers 15, 30, and 45, you may want to continue teaching time on the half hour and quarter hour. Draw a large circle on the board and divide it into four quarters. Shade the first quarter of the clock and show how it represents 15 minutes of time. Do the same for the half hour and three-quarter hour. Say: *It's (three) o'clock. It's three fifteen. It's three thirty. It's three forty-five. Now it's four o'clock.*

### 🎧 USING PAGE 53

Help students find page 53 in their books. Play the recording or read the words as you point to each. Model complete sentences for students and ask them to repeat as you point to each Picture Card: *I (wake up).*

Ask students to listen and follow the directions.

*I wake up. Draw a red circle.*
*I go to sleep. Draw an orange circle.*
*I go to school. Draw a yellow circle.*
*I eat breakfast. Draw a green circle.*
*Find the lunch. Draw a blue circle.*
*Find the dinner. Draw a purple circle.*
*I get dressed. Draw a brown circle.*
*I listen to music. Draw a red circle.*
*I play the piano. Draw an orange circle.*
*I go home. Draw a black circle.*

**Simple Present, *When...?*    53**

## USING PAGE 54

Help students find page 54 in their books. Play the recording or read the Grammar Box. As you listen to or read each sentence, point to the activity. Explain that we use the preposition *at* before the exact time when we are telling what we do and when we do it. We use the simple present to tell about activities we do all the time, every day.

Read the directions for the activity and ask students to read with you. Ask students to identify each action represented by the pictures. Read the first sentence and explain that the words *I eat dinner* best finish that sentence. Ask students to trace the words. Use a similar procedure to complete the page with students. When students have finished, write the sentences on the board so they can self-check their work.

### HAVING FUN!
#### Make a Paper Plate Clock

Model how to make the clock. Students work in pairs. Give each student a paper plate, brad or butterfly clip, scissors, and markers or crayons. Show them how to write the numerals *1–12* around the face of the clock. Give each group a template for the minute hand and the hour hand and a piece of cardboard. Show students how to trace the hands and cut them out. Help them fasten the hands in the center of the clock using the brad or butterfly clip. The hour hand goes on the bottom. The minute hand goes on the top. Give directions and ask students to set their clocks: *It's 6:00.* After they set their clocks, ask: *What time is it?* Students reply. Model if necessary. Continue the activity, asking students to set their clocks to the hour, half hour, and quarter hour. Invite students to take turns being the teacher. Let them give directions to each other.

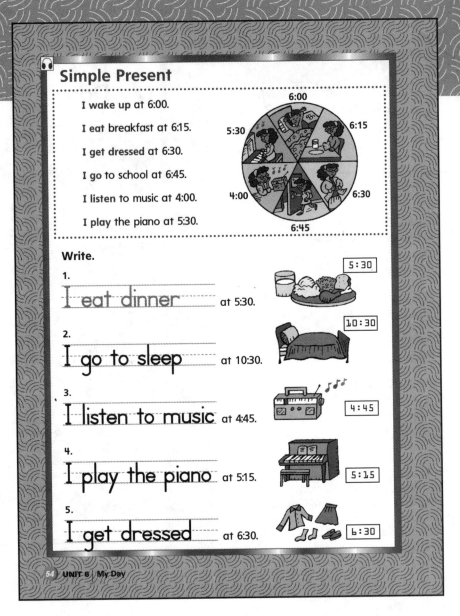

### Time Race

Use the clocks students prepared in the activity above. Say a time, using the hour, quarter hour, or half hour. Students work as quickly as they can to set their clocks. The student who sets his or her clock correctly first gets to say the next time. Students can race each other as a class or race in pairs.

### A Listening Activity

Model the activity. Ask students to form a line from the front to the back of the room. Place a toy clock or a paper plate clock on the board. Whisper a time to the first student in line. Motion for the first student to whisper the time to the next student in line. Students continue whispering the time until the last student is

reached. This student says the time and then sets the clock. The first student verifies if he or she is correct. When students are playing, change their places in line so that each student gets to be either the first or last student. You may want to form more than one line so that more students can participate at one time.

### Three in a Row

Give each student one set of Picture Cards. Model the activity. Say three activities: *I get dressed. I go to school. I listen to music.* Students say the activities in the same order and then place the Picture Cards in the order in which you said them. Model complete sentences and ask students to use complete sentences while playing.

**Vocabulary:** eat breakfast, eat dinner, eat lunch, get dressed, go home, go to school, go to sleep, listen to music, play the piano, wake up

### Lesson Objectives
✓ to identify daily activities

✓ to tell time to the hour, half hour, and quarter hour

✓ to use the simple present tense with *I, he, she*

### Classroom English
• Find. Say. Color. Draw. Write. Show me. What do you do? What time is it?

### Language Patterns
• I (eat lunch) at (12:30).

• (He/She) (plays the piano).

• I (get dressed).

### Materials
• Index cards with these times: 1:00, 2:30, 3:15, 4:45, 5:00, 6:30, 7:15, 8:45, 9:00, 9:30, 10:15, 11:45, 12:00; index cards with clock faces drawn for each of the listed times; drawing paper; crayons; markers; index cards with words: *he, she, I*

• **Picture Cards:** wake up, go to sleep, go to school, eat breakfast, eat lunch, eat dinner, get dressed, listen to music, play the piano, go home

## WARMING UP

Show students the Picture Cards and review the actions. Draw a large clock on the board and draw different times for the hour, half hour, and quarter hour. Model each time for students and ask them to say the times with you.

Invite a boy to come up. Whisper an action to him and ask him to act it out. Invite the rest of the class to guess which action it is. Model the sentence: *He (wakes up)*. Invite other boys to come up. Practice saying sentences using *he* plus the simple present for the actions in this unit. Emphasize the final *-s* (or *-es*) ending on the third

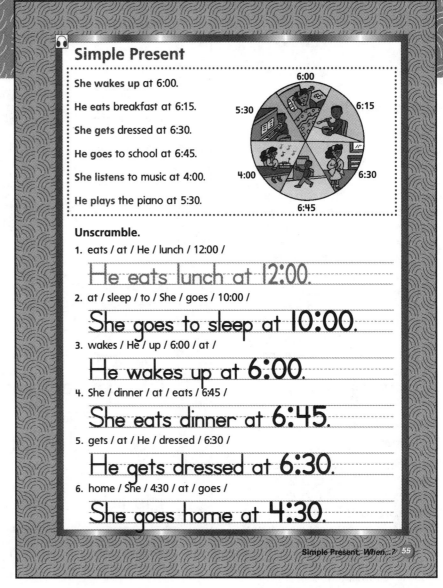

### Simple Present

She wakes up at 6:00.

He eats breakfast at 6:15.

She gets dressed at 6:30.

He goes to school at 6:45.

She listens to music at 4:00.

He plays the piano at 5:30.

**Unscramble.**

1. eats / at / He / lunch / 12:00 /

   He eats lunch at 12:00.

2. at / sleep / to / She / goes / 10:00 /

   She goes to sleep at 10:00.

3. wakes / He / up / 6:00 / at /

   He wakes up at 6:00.

4. She / dinner / at / eats / 6:45 /

   She eats dinner at 6:45.

5. gets / at / He / dressed / 6:30 /

   He gets dressed at 6:30.

6. home / She / 4:30 / at / goes /

   She goes home at 4:30.

*Simple Present, When...?* 55

person singular form of the verb. Write these examples on the board and underline the final *-s* at the end of the verb. Ask students to read with you.

Repeat the activity. Ask girls to act out the actions. Model sentences and ask students to repeat: *She (plays the piano)*. Emphasize the final *-s*. Write these examples on the board and underline the final *-s* at the end of the verb. Ask students to read with you.

##  USING PAGE 55

Help students find page 55 in their books. Ask students to identify the actions. Play the recording or read the Grammar Box. Explain that when we talk about another person doing actions all the time, every day, we use

*he/she* plus the action. The action word has a final *-s* or *-es* at the end.

Read the directions for the activity and ask students to follow along. Read each word of the first scrambled sentence. Explain to students that the words are not in the correct order and that they will be rewriting the sentence in the correct order. Read the unscrambled sentence with students and ask them to trace the sentence. Use a similar procedure to complete the page with students. Write the new sentence on the board for students so they can self-check their work.

## USING PAGE 56

Help students find page 56 in their books. Help them find Exercise A. Ask them to identify the actions in the picture. Explain that students will be matching each action in the picture with the words that describe it. Show students how the arrow leads from number 1 to the matching illustration. Complete the page with students. Now help them find Exercise B. Tell them that the words and objects above the sentences are clues to writing the sentences. Help them to see that the clues in number 1 match the sentence. Tell them to trace the sentence and then use a similar procedure to complete the page with them.

## HAVING FUN!
### Time Matching

Write the following times on index cards ahead of time: *1:00, 2:30, 3:15, 4:45, 5:00, 6:30, 7:15, 8:45, 9:00, 9:30, 10:15, 11:45, 12:00.* Draw clocks to represent these times on a separate set of index cards. Show students the times and ask them to tell what time it is. Show students the clocks and ask them to identify the times. Place the clock index cards facedown on one side of a table or floor. Place the time Picture Cards facedown on the other side of the table or floor. Model the activity. Students take turns turning over one card from each set of index cards. Encourage them to say the times. If the clock matches the time, they keep the pair. If not, play goes to the next student. Students play until all the pairs are found. The student with the most pairs at the end of the game wins. You may want to make several sets of cards so that more students can participate at one time.

### Make Sentences

Write the following words on index cards: *he, she, I.* Place the index cards

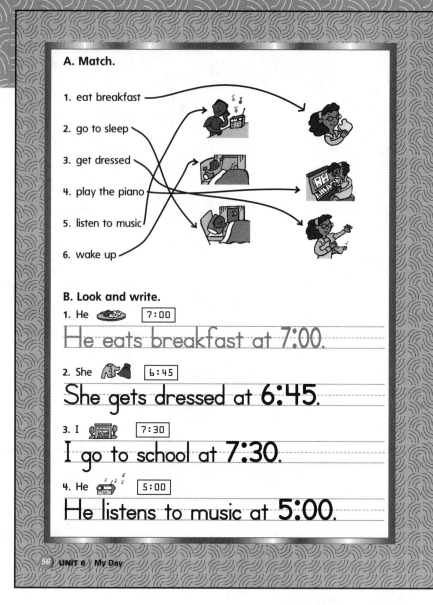

in one pile. Place the Picture Cards in a second pile. Model the activity. Students take turns choosing one index card and one Picture Card. Students make and say sentences. For example, if students choose *he* and *wake up*, they say the sentence: *He wakes up.* Continue playing until each student has had a turn. For an added challenge, include a third pile with times: *He wakes up at 6:30.*

### My Favorite Activity

Hold up a Picture Card representing your favorite activity and explain that you like to do it. Draw a simple picture of your favorite activity and label it with the corresponding action. Draw a clock to show when you do the activity. Show the picture and

clock to students and explain that students will be drawing pictures of their favorite activities, labeling them, and drawing a clock in the picture to show when they do the activity. Give each student a piece of drawing paper, crayons, and markers. When their pictures are finished, invite individual students to share their pictures with the rest of the class. Ask them to say a sentence about their pictures: *I play the piano at 2:00.* Model sentences if necessary.

**Vocabulary:** eat breakfast, eat dinner, eat lunch, get dressed, go home, go to school, go to sleep, listen to music, play the piano, wake up

### Lesson Objectives
✓ to identify daily actions

✓ to tell time to the hour, half hour, and quarter hour

✓ to use the simple present tense with *I, you, he, she*

✓ to ask and answer questions with *when*

### Classroom English
• Find. Say. Color. Draw. Write. Show me. What do you do? What time is it?

### Language Patterns
• When do you (get up)?

• I (get up) at (7:00).

• When does (he/she) eat lunch?

• (He/She) (eats lunch) at (12:30).

### Materials
• Game boards prepared with poster board; index cards with numerals *0, 1, 2* written three times each; one set of Picture Cards for each student; drawing or construction paper; slips of paper with the actions: *wake up, go to sleep, go to school, eat breakfast, lunch, dinner, get dressed, listen to music, play the piano, go home*

• **Picture Cards:** wake up, go to sleep, go to school, eat breakfast, eat lunch, eat dinner, get dressed, listen to music, play the piano, go home

## WARMING UP

Draw a clock on the board that shows *12:30*. Add a picture of a girl to the board. Show students the Picture Card: *eat lunch.* Ask the question and model the response: *When does she eat lunch? She eats lunch at 12:30.* Students repeat. Continue with additional examples that use the actions from this unit. Write the questions and answers on the board and read them with students. Explain

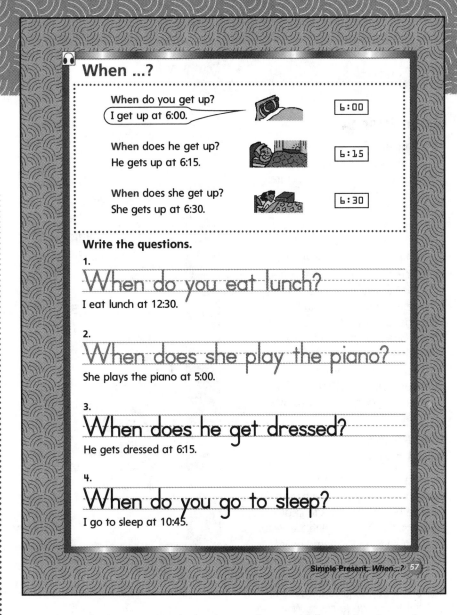

that we use the question word *when* to ask the time that someone does an action. Remind students when to use the final *-s* at the end of the action for the simple present tense responses.

## 🎧 USING PAGE 57

Help students find page 57 in their books. Play the recording or read the Grammar Box. Ask students to read with you. Remind students that we use the question word *when* to ask the time that someone does an action. Read the directions for the activity. Read number 1, ask students to read with you, and then ask them to trace the question. Repeat the procedure for number 2. Ask students

what word follows *when* in number 1 and what word follows *when* in number 2. Explain that *does* is used when the answer contains *he* or *she*. Use a similar procedure to complete the page with students. Write the questions on the board so students can self-check their work.

## USING PAGE 58

Help students find page 58 in their books. Ask students to identify the actions represented by the pictures. Read number 1 with students and explain that they should draw the time on the clock to show when they do the activity. Students trace and then write words to complete the sentence and fill in the corresponding time. Use a similar procedure to complete the page with students. Write the first part of each sentence on the board so students can self-check their work. When students are finished, ask them to sit in pairs and to ask and answer: *When do you (wake up)? I (wake up) at (6:30).*

## HAVING FUN!
### Board Game

Use the Picture Cards from this unit and a piece of poster board to make a game board for each group of students. Cut out and glue the Picture Cards in an *S* on the game board. Arrange the Picture Cards so they show, in order, what we usually do during the day. Begin with *wake up* and finish with *go to sleep*. Write the numerals *0, 1, 2* on index cards three times so you have nine cards. Use pieces of paper or colored paper clips as game pieces. Play the game in groups of three or four. Model how the game is played. Shuffle the numeral cards and place them facedown on the table. Students take turns turning over the top numeral card and moving their game piece *zero, one,* or *two* spaces. Students identify the action they land on and say a sentence: *I ( wake up) at (7:00).* The student to get to the finish line *go to sleep* first, wins.

### Picture Card Bingo

Prepare a sample Bingo grid ahead of time with Picture Cards from this unit pasted into the spaces. Show students

the finished Bingo grid. Give each student a piece of paper and a set of Picture Cards from this unit. Show students how to make their own Bingo grids by pasting Picture Cards in the nine spaces. Tell students that everyone's Bingo grid should be different. One space should be labeled *Free.* Use paper clips or small pieces of paper for markers. Call out daily activities randomly. Students place markers on the pictures. Three in a row wins. The winner says a sentence for each word in the winning row.

### Write the Times

Give each student a piece of drawing paper and show him or her how to fold it into eight spaces. Explain and model the activity. Students write the

times and draw corresponding clocks as you say them. Say the following times: *1:00, 2:30, 3:45, 4:15, 5:00, 6:15, 12:00, 11:15.* When students are finished, write the times and draw the clocks on the board so students can self-check their work.

### Act It Out

Write the following actions on slips of paper ahead of time: *wake up, go to sleep, go to school, eat breakfast, eat lunch, eat dinner, get dressed, listen to music, play the piano, go home.* Read each one with students. Fold the slips of paper and place them in a box or bag. Model the activity. Students take turns choosing a slip of paper and acting out the action. The student who guesses correctly first gets to be the next actor.

**Vocabulary:** eat breakfast, eat dinner, eat lunch, get dressed, go home, go to school, go to sleep, listen to music, play the piano, wake up

**Lesson Objectives**
- ✓ to identify daily activities
- ✓ to tell time to the hour, half hour, and quarter hour
- ✓ to use the simple present tense
- ✓ to ask and answer questions with *when*

**Classroom English**
- Play. Show me. Find. Say. What do you do? What time is it? What is it? It's (dinner).

**Language Patterns**
- When do you (wake up)?
- I (wake up) at (7:00).

**Materials**
- **Picture Cards:** wake up, go to sleep, go to school, eat breakfast, eat lunch, eat dinner, get dressed, listen to music, play the piano, go home

## WARMING UP

Review vocabulary from this unit by showing students the Picture Cards and asking them to identify the actions. Model if necessary. Write different times that show the hour, half hour, and quarter hour on the board. Ask students to say the times with you. Practice asking and answering questions with *when: When do you (eat dinner)? I (eat dinner) at (6:00).*

## USING PAGE 59

Help students find page 59 in their books. Play the recording or read the chant for students. Point to each Picture Card as the word appears in the chant. Invite a student to fill in the times during the chant. Model and ask students to follow along and point to each word as they listen. After students have listened to and read

**Chant.**

When do you wake up?
When do you wake up?
I wake up at 7:00.
I wake up at 7:00.

When do you get dressed?
When do you get dressed?
I get dressed at 7:30.
I get dressed at 7:30.

When do you eat lunch?
When do you eat lunch?
I eat lunch at 1:00.
I eat lunch at 1:00.

Simple Present, When...? 59

the chant a few times, invite them to say it with you. Encourage students to point to each word as they read. Place the corresponding Picture Cards on the board. Say the chant again and invite students to come up and point to the corresponding Picture Cards and to fill in a time as the chant is said.

## EXTENSION
### Continue the Chant

Review the chant with students by playing the recording or reading it for them. Substitute other actions. Students say the new chant. Invite volunteers to come up and point to the corresponding Picture Cards as they hear them in the chant and to fill in a time.

### Act Out the Chant

Review the chant with students by playing the recording or reading it for them. Ask students to role-play the actions during the chant.

### Take the Parts

Divide the class into two groups. Groups alternate asking and answering the questions.

**Vocabulary:** eat breakfast, eat dinner, eat lunch, get dressed, go home, go to school, go to sleep, listen to music, play the piano, wake up

**Lesson Objective**
✓ to identify daily activities

**Classroom English**
• Play. Show me. Find. Say. Write. What do you do?

**Language Pattern**
• I (eat lunch) at 12:45.

**Materials**
• Crayons and pencils or markers, drawing paper, large pieces of poster board
• **Picture Cards:** wake up, play the piano, go to sleep, go to school, eat lunch, get dressed

## WARMING UP

Show students the Picture Cards for this unit and review the actions with them. As you say each action, write it on the board and read it with students. Invite students to use each action in a sentence: *I (play the piano) at 4:00.*

## USING PAGE 60

Help students find page 60. Ask students to identify the actions represented by each picture. Show students how each phrase matches its corresponding picture. Show students the crossword puzzle and explain that they will be writing the actions for each picture. Point out that the numbers in the puzzle correspond to the numbers with the pictures. The words either go across or down. Students write one letter in each box. Complete the crossword puzzle with students. Write the answers on the board, crossword style, so students can self-check their work.

---

**A. Look and say.**

wake up

play the piano

go to school

eat lunch

get dressed

go to sleep

**B. Write the words.**

1. W
2. P L A Y  T H E  P I A N O
3. G O T O S L E E P (6. across)
4. E A T  L U N C H
5. G
6. GO TO SLEEP

Down 1: WAKE UP
Down 3: GO TO SCHOOL
Down 5: GET DRESSED

UNIT 6 | My Day

---

## EXTENSION
### Make Your Own Crossword Puzzle

After students have completed their crossword puzzles, show them how to make a crossword of their own. Give each student a piece of drawing paper, crayons, and markers. Students draw picture clues for their crossword puzzles and boxes for each letter. Show students how to connect the words in their puzzles. When students are finished, ask them to write the answers to their crossword puzzles on a separate piece of paper. Students then switch papers with a partner and complete their partner's puzzle. When they are finished, students can share their answers with their partners.

## Activity Murals

Ahead of time, prepare a mural of daily activities. Show students the completed mural and ask them to identify the actions and tell when they are done. Students should use the simple present tense with *I, he, she.* Ask students to work in groups of three or four. Give each group of students a large piece of poster board. Students draw pictures of what they do in school every day and then draw a clock to show when they do the activity. When their murals are finished, invite each group to come up and talk about their murals. Encourage them to use the simple present tense with *I, you, he, she.*

**60 UNIT 6 My Day**

# Units 5 & 6
Review

**Vocabulary:** clerk, cook, dentist, doctor, eat breakfast, eat dinner, eat lunch, firefighter, get dressed, go home, go to school, go to sleep, librarian, listen to music, mail carrier, nurse, play the piano, police officer, teacher, vet, wake up

**Review Objectives**
✓ to identify community helpers
✓ to identify daily activities

**Classroom English**
• Listen. Check. Point. Say.

**Language Patterns**
• What does (he/she) do?
• (He's) a (doctor).
• I (eat dinner) at (7:30).

**Materials**
• **Picture Cards:** doctor, nurse, police officer, firefighter, cook, dentist, vet, mail carrier, librarian, teacher, clerk, wake up, go to sleep, go to school, eat breakfast, lunch, dinner, get dressed, listen to music, play the piano, go home

## WARMING UP

Review the occupations from Unit 5 by using the Picture Cards and asking: *What does (he/she) do?* Invite students to use a complete sentence when answering: *(He/She) is a (doctor).* Invite students to ask and answer questions as you hold up the Picture Cards. Model if necessary.

Review the actions. Hold up one of

the activity Picture Cards from Unit 6. Ask students to tell what the person does. Model responses if necessary: *(He) (gets dressed) (at 7:30).*

Tape a row of occupation Picture Cards to the board and write *yes* and *no* under each Picture Card. Draw a small box next to each of the words

*yes* and *no.* Point to each Picture Card and ask students to identify the occupations. Point to a card and say: *(She's) a (doctor).* Students should verify if the sentence you said is correct or incorrect according to the picture. Show students how to place a check in that box. Provide additional

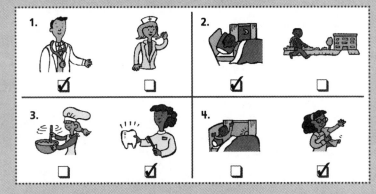

## Review: Units 5 and 6

### Vocabulary
🎧 **A. Listen and check.**

### What...?
🎧 **B. Listen and check.**

---

### AUDIOSCRIPT

**A.** 1. doctor    2. go to sleep    3. dentist    4. get dressed

**B.** 1. A: What does she do?      2. A: What does he do?      3. A: What does she do?
     B: She's a cook.           B: He's a firefighter.           B: She's a police officer.

    4. A: What does she do?      5. A: What does he do?      6. A: What does he do?
      B: She's a librarian.           B: He's a vet.           B: He's a teacher.

examples for students that allow them to check the *yes* and *no* boxes.

If you feel students need practice exercises that are similar to those presented in the Review Units, use exercises like the two previous ones so students can practice checking boxes and pictures that go with stated sentences and words. You can use similar exercises for any of the Review Exercises at the end of a unit.

## USING PAGE 61

Help students find page 61 in their books. Help students find Exercise A. Read the directions and ask students to follow along. Point to each picture and ask students to say the words with you. Explain to students that they should check the picture that goes with the word they hear. Play the recording or read the audioscript for students. Students check the correct picture.

Help students find Exercise B. Read the directions and ask students to follow along. Point to the pictures and ask students to tell you what each person does. Explain that they should check the *yes* box if the picture goes with what they hear. They should check the *no* box if the picture does not go with what they hear.

## USING PAGE 62

Help students find page 62 in their books. Help students find Exercise C. Read the directions and ask students to follow along. Point to each picture

### Review: Units 5 and 6

#### Simple Present
🎧 C. Listen and check.

#### Simple Present
🎧 D. Listen, point, and say.

62  Review | Units 5 and 6

and ask students to say the words with you. Explain to students that they should check the picture that goes with the sentence they hear. Play the recording or read the audioscript for students. Students check the correct picture.

Help students find Exercise D. Read the directions and ask students to follow along. Explain that they should

listen, point to the picture, and then say the sentence. Play the recording or read the audioscript for students.

---

### *AUDIOSCRIPT*

**C.** 1. I eat dinner at 7:30.
    3. I play the piano at four o'clock.
    2. I eat lunch at 12:30.
    4. I go to sleep at eight o'clock.

**D.** 1. She wakes up at six o'clock.  2. He eats lunch at 11:30.  3. He goes to school at 8:15.
    4. She east breakfast at 7:20.  5. They get dressed at 6:15.  6. She listens to music at 5:45.

# Unit 7
Food

## Count and Noncount Nouns, *Some*

**Vocabulary:** bread, carrot, cheese, chicken, fish, mango, onion, orange, potato, rice, soup, tomato, water

### Lesson Objectives
✓ to identify foods
✓ to say and write the plurals for some food words
✓ to tell how many food items one wants

### Classroom English
• Find. Say. Circle. Color. Draw. Write. Show me. What do you want?

### Language Patterns
• I want a (tomato).
• I want an (orange).
• I want (four) (carrots).

### Materials
• Crayons, markers, drawing paper, scissors, multiple copies of Picture Cards
• **Picture Cards:** chicken, soup, cheese, tomato, potato, carrot, onion, rice, bread, mango, orange, water

## WARMING UP

Show students Picture Cards for each food item. Introduce one Picture Card at a time. Ask students to repeat the new words after you say each one. Play a Show Me game with students. Place all the Picture Cards on the board, floor, or table in front of students. Say: *Show me the (cheese).* Students take turns pointing to the picture you named.

Make multiple copies of the Picture Cards. After students are familiar with the new vocabulary, show them more than one of each of these foods: *tomato, potato, carrot, onion, mango, orange.* Ask students to count the items with you. Explain that these items can be counted and we can make them plural. Write the singular form for each food item on the board and read the list with students. Now

Food

UNIT 7

water, potato, fish, onion, bread, tomato, carrot, orange, cheese, rice, chicken, mango, soup

*Plural and Noncount Nouns, Some* 63

hold up more than one of each food as you write the plurals in a second column. Read the plurals with students. Point out the irregular spellings for *tomatoes, potatoes,* and *mangos.* (*Mango* can be spelled *mangos* or *mangoes.*)

Hold up one of the food items and model the sentence: *I want a (tomato).* Ask students to repeat. Continue the activity with similar singular examples. Write the examples on the board and ask students to read with you.

Hold up more than one of the same food Picture Cards and model the sentence: *I want (two) (mangoes).* Continue the activity with similar plural examples. Write these on the board and ask students to read with you.

## 🎧 USING PAGE 63

Show students how to find page 63 in their books. Play the recording or read the words as you point to each. Allow students to talk about the pictures and encourage them to identify the food items. As you say each new word, point to the corresponding picture and ask students to repeat.

You may want to make a chart on the board of student likes and dislikes. Write the names of the foods on the board and then ask for a show of hands. Point to the pictured food as you say: *Do you like (chicken)?* Count the number of raised hands and write the number next to the word on the board. Continue for the other items.

Help students find page 64 in their books. Play the recording or read the Grammar Box as you point to the singular and plural food words. Explain that many plural nouns in English end in -s *(carrots, onions)*. Others end in -es *(tomatoes, potatoes)*.

Read the directions for the activity and ask students to follow along. Ask students to identify the food items in the pictures. Read the first sentence and explain that since there is reference to only one onion, the noun does not have a final -s. Explain to students that they are going to form a new sentence. Invite students to count the number of onions in the picture (three). Because there are three onions, *onion* needs to be changed to the plural form by adding a final -s. Ask students to trace the second sentence in number 1. Use a similar procedure to complete the rest of the page. Draw students' attention to the number in parentheses under the writing lines so that they understand what number to write in their sentences. Write the answers on the board so students can self-check their work.

## Having Fun!
### I Want

Make multiple copies of the following Picture Cards: *tomato, potato, carrot, mango, orange*. Model the sentence: *I want (four) oranges*. Ask students to repeat. Invite individuals to come up, choose a food, and tell how many they want. Encourage them to use sentences like the one you modeled.

### Drawing Dictation

Model the activity. Give each student a piece of drawing paper and show them how to fold it into eight spaces. Give the following directions:

1. *Draw a tomato.*
2. *Draw four potatoes.*
3. *Draw three carrots.*

4. *Draw an onion.*
5. *Draw five oranges.*
6. *Draw a mango.*
7. *Draw six onions.*
8. *Draw three tomatoes.*

When students are finished, ask them to color their pictures and to say a sentence about each one. For example: *I want (three) tomatoes*.

### A Listening Game

Place multiple copies of the following Picture Cards on the board: *tomato, potato, carrot, onion, mango, orange*. Ask students to identify each one and then ask them to say the plural forms as you hold up more than one of each food. Ask students to form a line from the front to the back of the room. Whisper a sentence to the first

student in line: *I want (five) (oranges)*. Motion for the first student to whisper the sentence to the second student. Students continue whispering the sentence until the last student is reached. The last student says the sentence and then picks up the correct number of Picture Cards of the food item. The first student verifies if he or she is correct. As students are playing, change their places in line so they get to be either the first or last student. You may want to form more than one line so that more students can participate at one time.

**Vocabulary:** bread, carrot, cheese, chicken, fish, mango, onion, orange, potato, rice, soup, tomato, water

### Lesson Objectives
✓ to identify food items

✓ to identify, say, and write the plurals of some food words

✓ to say and write noncount nouns that do not have a plural form

✓ to use the quantifier *some* for noncount food items

✓ to use a number to tell how many of a food item they want

### Classroom English
• Find. Say. Color. Draw. Write. Show me. What do you want? What do you like? Do you like (onions)?

### Language Patterns
• I want (two) mangoes.

• I want some (chicken).

### Materials
• Paper plates, plastic spoons or plastic forks, napkins, play money, lunch bags, drawing paper, crayons, markers

• **Realia:** foods from this unit for students to taste

• **Picture Cards:** chicken, soup, cheese, tomato, potato, carrot, onion, rice, bread, mango, orange, water

## WARMING UP

Show students the following Picture Cards and ask students to identify each food: *tomato, potato, carrot, onion, mango, orange.* Show them more than one of each food and ask them to use the plural form when telling what they see. Explain that we can count these foods. Model sentences such as: *I want (four) (mangoes). I want a (tomato).* Ask students to repeat. Write these sentences on the board and read them with students.

Now show students the following Picture Cards and explain that we

**Noncount Nouns**

Some nouns can be counted.

I want three potatoes.

Some nouns cannot be counted. They do not have a plural form.

I want some chicken.

**Write.**

1.

I want some water.
(water)

2.

I want some bread.
(bread)

3.

I want some rice.
(rice)

Plural and Noncount Nouns, *Some* 65

usually do not count them: *chicken, soup, cheese, rice, bread, water.* Show students multiple pictures for each word and explain that the words do not have a plural form. Model sentences and ask students to repeat: *I want some (rice).* Write the sentences on the board and read them with students.

## USING PAGE 65

Help students find page 65 in their books. Play the recording or read the Grammar Box. Explain that some nouns in English are usually not counted. Point out that we do not use a number before a noun we cannot count.

Read the directions for the activity and ask students to read with you. Ask students to identify the food items in each picture. Read the sentence in number 1. Point to the word *water* in parentheses. Explain that *water* cannot be counted. Read the sentence again with students and ask them to trace it. Help students to complete the page. Write the answers on the board so students can self-check their work.

## USING PAGE 66

Help students find page 66 in their books. Read the directions for the exercise and ask students to read with you. Ask them to identify each food. Explain that they will be completing each sentence with the word represented by the picture. Do number 1 with students, asking them which word is needed to complete the sentence. Invite them to write *rice* on the line. Use a similar procedure to complete the page. Write the answers on the board so students can self-check their work.

## HAVING FUN
### Sorting

Use the food Picture Cards for this game. Place two bags on a table or on the floor in front of students. Label one bag *noncount* and draw a picture of a bowl of soup on it. Label the other bag *count* and draw an orange on it. Show students the Picture Cards and ask them to identify the foods. Place the Picture Cards in a pile. Divide the class into two teams. Students from each team take turns choosing a card and putting it in the correct bag. Students score one point for each correct answer. The team with the most points at the end of the game wins.

### Play Store

Use real food items or the food Picture Cards for this game. Provide play money and lunch bags to put the food in. Model the activity. Students take turns being the store keeper and the customer. Model a short conversation and ask students to practice it before playing:

Store Keeper: *What do you want?*
Customer: *I want (some) (rice) and a (mango).*
Store Keeper: *Two dollars, please.*

(Puts the food in a bag.)
Customer (hands store keeper the money): *Thank you.*
Store Keeper: *You're welcome.*

Encourage students to ask for more than one item when playing. Encourage them to use complete sentences when asking and responding.

### Play Restaurant

Play the above game again, but change the setting to a restaurant. Model the activity. The waiter or waitress writes the customer's order on a piece of paper and then brings it to him or her, using realia or the food Picture Cards. Provide paper plates, plastic forks, and spoons.

### Find It First

Show students the food Picture Cards from this unit and ask them to identify each one. Place the Picture Cards on the board or on the floor in front of students. Divide the class into two teams and ask each team to form a line from the front to the back of the room. Say one of the food words. The first student in each line walks as fast as he or she can to the Picture Cards, picks up the correct one, and says the word. Teams receive one point for each correct response. Students can receive a bonus point if they can use the word in a sentence. The team with the most points at the end of the game wins.

**Vocabulary:** bread, carrot, cheese, chicken, fish, mango, onion, orange, potato, rice, soup, tomato, water

### Lesson Objectives
✓ to identify foods

✓ to say and write the plurals for some food words

✓ to use count and noncount food words

✓ to use the quantifier *some*

✓ to use numbers for exact amounts

✓ to use *there is* and *there are* for count and noncount food items

### Classroom English
• Find. Say. Color. Draw. Write. Show me. What do you want?

### Language Patterns
• I want (some) (cheese).

• I want (three) (mangoes).

• There is (an) (onion) (on the table).

### Materials
• Scrambled words on index cards: *hicieckn (chicken), ifhs (fish), puos (soup), hcesee (cheese), otmoat (tomato), opttao (potato), trcaro (carrot), onoin (onion), crie (rice), drbea (bread), nmaog (mango), aorneg (orange), twaer (water);* multiple copies of Picture Cards; tape

• **Picture Cards:** chicken, soup, cheese, tomato, potato, carrot, onion, rice, bread, mango, orange, water

**Some**

Use **some** with plural nouns and noncount nouns.

I want some oranges.    I want some chicken.

**Write and match.**

1. I want some bread. (bread)

2. I want some rice. (rice)

3. I want some onions. (onion)

4. I want some soup. (soup)

## WARMING UP

Use multiple copies of the Picture Cards. Write the words *There is* on the board to form one column. Write the words *There are* on the board to form a second column. Show students one of each Picture Card and ask them to identify each food item. Use each word in a sentence with *there is: There is (a) (tomato). There is (some) (rice).* Ask students to say each sentence with you and then tape each Picture Card under the *There is* column. Explain that we

use *There is* for singular count nouns and noncount nouns.

Now show students multiple copies of the following Picture Cards: *tomato, potato, carrot, onion, mango, orange.* Model sentences with *there are: There are (five) (tomatoes).* Ask students to say these sentences with you. Tape multiple copies of these Picture Cards under the second column. Explain that we use *there are* for plural nouns.

## 🎧 USING PAGE 67

Help students find page 67 in their books. Play the recording or read the Grammar Box. Explain that we use the word *some* with plural nouns and noncount nouns.

Read the directions for the activity and ask students to read with you. Read the word *bread* in number 1, and then read the sentence *I want some bread.* Ask students to trace the words in the sentence, and then show them how to draw a line from the sentence to the picture. Use a similar procedure to complete the page with students. Students write sentences for each word. Write the answers on the board so students can self-check their work.

## USING PAGE 68

Help students find page 68 in their books. Read the directions and ask students to read with you. Ask students to identify each food item on the page. Read each sentence with students and explain that they should draw a picture on the table at the bottom of the page for each sentence. Draw a table on the board and draw the pictures with students as you complete the page. When they are finished, ask students to first self-check their work and then talk about their pictures with a partner.

## HAVING FUN!

### Scrambled Words

Write the following scrambled words on index cards: *hcieckn (chicken), ifhs (fish), puos (soup), hcesee (cheese), otmoat (tomato), opttao (potato), trcaro (carrot), onoin (onion), crie (rice), drbea (bread), nmaog (mango), aorneg (orange), twaer (water)*. Write the food vocabulary words on the board for students to use as a reference. Show students the first index card. Students work as fast as they can to unscramble the word. The student who does this correctly first gets a point. Students win a bonus point if they use the word in a sentence. Students then tape the index card next to the corresponding word on the board. Continue playing until all the words are unscrambled. The student with the most points at the end of the game wins.

### What's Missing?

Use multiple copies of the Picture Cards but do not use more than twelve Picture Cards at a time. Place these Picture Cards on the floor or on a table in front of students. Ask students to first identify each food item and then to point out if there is more than one of a food item. Ask

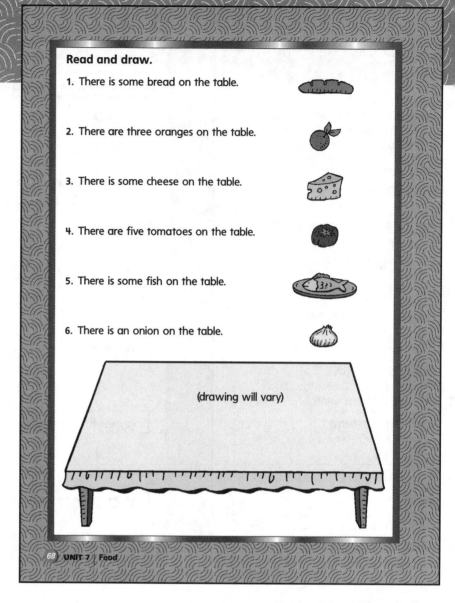

**Read and draw.**

1. There is some bread on the table.

2. There are three oranges on the table.

3. There is some cheese on the table.

4. There are five tomatoes on the table.

5. There is some fish on the table.

6. There is an onion on the table.

(drawing will vary)

68 UNIT 7 Food

students to close their eyes. Take away either one or more than one of a food item. Ask students to open their eyes and to tell what is missing. Students use the correct form of the noun, singular or plural, when answering.

### Following Directions

Give each student a piece of drawing paper and show them how to draw a large table in the center of the page. Ask them to listen and follow directions. Students draw pictures as you say the sentences:

1. *There is a tomato on the table.*
2. *There are five oranges on the table.*
3. *There is some cheese on the table.*
4. *There are two onions on the table.*
5. *There is some water on the table.*
6. *There is some fish on the table.*
7. *There are six carrots on the table.*
8. *There are four mangoes on the table.*

Draw a table on the board. After students are finished with their pictures, ask them to tell what is on the table, using sentences with *there is* and *there are*. Draw pictures on the table on the board and ask students to self-check their work. Then, ask students to color their pictures and to add more food items to their pictures. Students then pick a partner and tell what is on their tables.

**Vocabulary:** bread, carrot, cheese, chicken, fish, mango, onion, orange, potato, rice, soup, tomato, water

**Lesson Objectives**
✓ to identify foods
✓ to say and write the plurals for some food words
✓ to use count and noncount food words
✓ to use the quantifier *some*
✓ to use numbers for exact amounts
✓ to tell what one wants

**Classroom English**
• Play. Show me. Find. Say. What do you want?

**Language Patterns**
• I want (some) (soup).
• I want (three) (mangoes).

**Materials**
• **Picture Cards:** chicken, soup, cheese, tomato, potato, carrot, onion, rice, bread, mango, orange, water

 Chant.

Cheese, cheese
I want some cheese.

Rice, rice
I want some rice.

Soup, soup
I want some soup.

Mangoes, mangoes
I want some mangoes.

Onions, onions
I want some onions.

Carrots, carrots
I want some carrots.

**Plural and Noncount Nouns,** *Some* 69

## WARMING UP

Review vocabulary from this unit by showing students the Picture Cards and asking them to identify the food words. Model if necessary. Draw a large table on the board and tape some of the Picture Cards on the table. Use more than one of some Picture Cards. Ask students to tell what is on the table. Students should use sentences with *There is* and *There are.*

## USING PAGE 69

Help students find page 69 in their books. Play the recording or read the chant for students. Point to each Picture Card as the word appears in the chant. Model and ask students to follow along and point to each word as they listen. After they have listened to and read the chant a few times,

invite students to say it with you. Encourage them to point to each word as they read. Place the corresponding Picture Cards on the board. Say the chant again and invite students to come up and point to the corresponding Picture Cards as they hear them in the chant.

## EXTENSION
### Continue the Chant

Review the chant with students by playing the recording or reading it for them. Substitute other food words and numbers where appropriate. Students say the new chant. Invite volunteers to come up and point to the corresponding Picture Cards as they hear them in the chant.

### Extend the Chant

Review the chant with students by playing the recording or reading it for them. Ask students to hold up the correct number of fingers when numbers appear in the chant.

### Take the Parts

Divide the class into two groups. Groups alternate saying the first and second lines of each stanza.

**Vocabulary:** bread, carrot, cheese, chicken, fish, mango, onion, orange, potato, rice, soup, tomato, water

### Lesson Objectives
✓ to identify foods
✓ to say and write the plurals for some food words
✓ to use count and noncount food words

### Classroom English
• Play. Show me. Find. Say. Write. Circle.

### Language Patterns
• There are (three) (carrots).
• There is (an) (onion).
• There is (some) (water).

### Materials
• Crayons and pencils or markers, drawing paper
• **Picture Cards:** chicken, soup, cheese, tomato, potato, carrot, onion, rice, bread, mango, orange, water

## WARMING UP

Show students the Picture Cards for this unit and review the food words with them. As you say each food word, write it on the board and read it with students. Invite students to use each food word in a sentence: *There is (an) (onion). There are (four) (carrots). There is some (cheese).*

## USING PAGE 70

Help students find page 70 in their books. Ask students to identify the food items pictured and to read each corresponding word. Ask them to look at the word search puzzle on the page. Explain that the words at the top of the page are hidden in the puzzle and go vertically and horizontally. Show students how to find and circle the words. Ask students to work in pairs to complete the puzzle. When they are finished,

---

**Find the words.**

oranges    water    cheese

onion    carrots   chicken

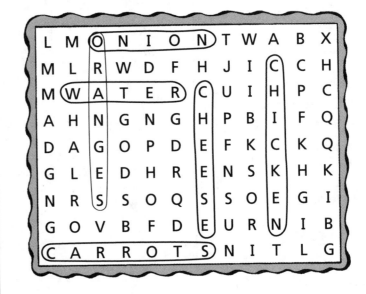

---

show them a completed puzzle so they can self-check their work.

## EXTENSION
### Make Your Own Word Search Puzzle

After students have completed their word search puzzles, show them how to make a word search of their own. Give them a piece of drawing paper, crayons, and markers. Students draw picture clues and write the words for their word search puzzles. Students then create their own word search puzzles by hiding words vertically and horizontally. Show students how to connect the words in their puzzles. When students are finished, ask them to switch papers with a partner and complete their partner's puzzle.

Students then ask their partners to check their work.

## Chicken

Write the word *chicken* vertically on the board. Show students how to connect other words to the word *chicken*. Have students work in pairs to connect as many food words as they can to the original word. The students with the largest number of correctly spelled food words win. For example:

**C**arrot
fis**H**
on**I**on
**C**heese
ca**K**e
br**E**ad
ma**N**go

---

# Unit 8
## At the Zoo

### Punctuation, *Have/Has*, *Its/Their*

**Vocabulary:** alligator, bear, elephant, giraffe, gorilla, hippo, lion, monkey, panda, seal, tiger, zebra

### WARMING UP

Show students Picture Cards for the following zoo animals: *alligator, bear, elephant, giraffe, gorilla, hippo, lion, monkey, panda, seal, tiger, zebra.* Introduce one Picture Card at a time. Ask students to repeat the new words after you say each one. Play a guessing game with students. Place all the Picture Cards on the floor or on a table in front of students. Ask them to identify each animal and then turn over the Picture Cards. Ask students to find the animals, one at a time. You can ask: *Where is the (elephant)?* Students take turns turning over one Picture Card. If they find the animal, they keep the Picture Card. The student with the most Picture Cards at the end of the game wins.

Hold up one of the zoo animal Picture Cards and look excited. Say in an excited way: *Look at the (zebra)!* Write this sentence on the board and point out that you used an

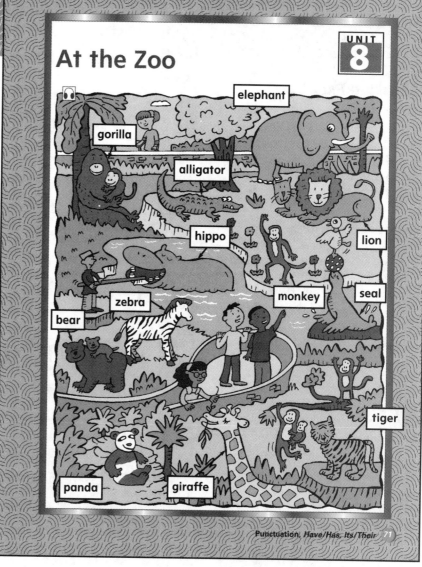

exclamation mark at the end of the sentence. Explain that the exclamation mark means that you are surprised or excited. Substitute other zoo animals into the sentence and write these on the board. Invite individual students to come up and add the exclamation mark at the end of each sentence.

You may want to make a chart on the board of students' likes and dislikes. Write the names of the zoo animals on the board and then ask for a show of hands. Point to the pictured animal as you say: *Do you like (zebras)?* Count the number of raised hands and write the number next to the zoo animal word on the board. Continue for the other animals.

###  USING PAGE 71

Help students find page 71 in their books. Play the recording or read the words. Allow students to talk about the pictures and encourage them to identify the zoo animals. As you say each new word, point to the corresponding picture and ask students to repeat.

## Using Page 72

Help students find page 72 in their books. Play the recording or read the Grammar Box as you point to the sentence and exclamation mark. Explain that we use an exclamation mark to show that we are surprised or excited.

Read the directions for the activity and ask students to read with you. Read the first sentence and the word in parentheses. Ask students to read with you and point out that they should sound excited because there is an exclamation mark at the end of the sentence. Ask students to trace the sentence and draw a picture of a gorilla. Use a similar procedure to complete the page. Students write a sentence with an exclamation mark for each word and draw the corresponding picture. Write the answers on the board so students can self-check their work.

## Having Fun!

### Act It Out

Write the animal names on slips of paper. Place them in a bag or box and invite students to take turns choosing one and then acting like the animal. The student who guesses first gets to be the next actor. As students are guessing, encourage them to say: *Look at the (gorilla)!*

### Drawing Dictation

Model the activity. Give each student a piece of drawing paper and show them how to fold it into eight spaces. Students can draw eight pictures on the front and three pictures on the back. Give the following directions:

1. *Draw a brown gorilla.*
2. *Draw a brown and white giraffe.*
3. *Draw a white bear.*
4. *Draw a brown monkey.*
5. *Draw an orange and black tiger.*
6. *Draw a yellow lion.*
7. *Draw a gray elephant.*
8. *Draw a green alligator.*
9. *Draw a black and white panda.*
10. *Draw a brown seal.*
11. *Draw a gray hippo.*

When students are finished, ask them to sit with a partner and talk about their pictures.

### Riddles

Place the Picture Cards on the board. Say each of the following riddles and ask students to guess which animal you are talking about. When students guess, ask them to say the animal name and point to the corresponding Picture Card. Students get one point for each correct answer. The student with the most points at the end of the game wins.

1. *I am brown. I am big. I have two hands and two feet. I have fingers and toes like you. (gorilla)*
2. *I am brown and white. I have a long neck. I eat leaves on trees. (giraffe)*
3. *I am black and white and I look like a horse. (zebra)*
4. *I am brown, white, or black. I am big. I can run fast. (bear)*
5. *I am small. I am brown. I eat bananas. (monkey)*
6. *I am black and orange. (tiger)*
7. *I am yellow or brown. I am big. I have a lot of hair. (lion)*
8. *I am gray. I have big ears. (elephant)*
9. *I am green. I swim in the water. (alligator)*

**Vocabulary:** alligator, bear, big, elephant, giraffe, gorilla, hippo, lion, long, monkey, panda, seal, short, small, tiger, zebra

**Lesson Objectives**
✓ to identify zoo animals
✓ to use *have* in simple present questions
✓ to use *has* in simple present responses
✓ to use adjectives to describe animals

**Classroom English**
• Find. Say. Color. Draw. Write. Show me. What is it?

**Language Patterns**
• What does a (lion) have?
• A (lion) has (big) (teeth).

**Materials**
• Animal names on index cards; body parts on index cards: *ears, nose, eyes, tail, teeth, arms, legs, neck, mouth;* paper plates; craft sticks
• **Picture Cards:** gorilla, giraffe, zebra, bear, monkey, tiger, lion, elephant, alligator, panda, seal, hippo

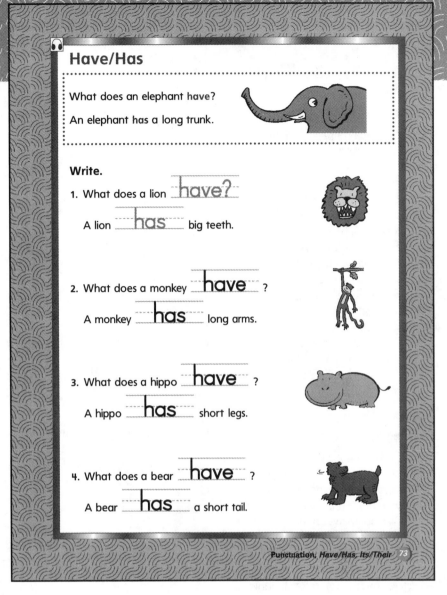

## Warming Up

Show students the following Picture Cards and ask students to identify each zoo animal: *gorilla, giraffe, zebra, bear, monkey, tiger, lion, elephant, alligator, panda, seal, hippo.* Review the adjectives: *big, small, long, short* with students. Draw a picture of a giraffe on the board and point to the giraffe's neck. Say: *The giraffe has a long neck.* Continue by drawing pictures of other animals and asking students to describe them using these adjectives. Model if necessary.

Now ask students: *What does a (giraffe) have?* Write the question on the board and ask students to read it with you. Underline the word *have* and point out that the question uses the word *have.* Now model the

response: *A (giraffe) has a (long) (neck).* Write this on the board and read it with students. Underline the word *has* and point out that when we use the name of an animal or *he, she, it,* the answer contains *has.* Continue the activity by providing similar examples. Use the zoo animals and adjectives students practiced. Write these on the board and read them with students.

## Using Page 73

Help students find page 73 in their books. Ask students to identify the elephant. Play the recording or read the Grammar Box. Explain that the question uses *have.* Explain that the response uses *has.*

Read the directions for the activity and ask students to read with you. Ask students to identify the animals. Read the question and answer in number 1 and ask students to read with you. Students trace the word *have* in the question and the word *has* in the response. Now ask students to find the lion. Use a similar procedure to complete the page with students. Write the answers on the board so students can self-check their work.

## USING PAGE 74

Help students find page 74 in their books. Read the directions for the activity and ask students to read with you. Ask students to identify the animals in each picture and to use adjectives to describe them. Read the first question with students and remind them that the question uses *have*. Ask students to read with you and trace the word *have* to complete the question. Read the answer and ask students to read with you. Students trace the answer. Use a similar procedure to complete the page with students. Write the answers on the board so students can self-check their work.

## HAVING FUN!
### Making Sentences

Write the following animal names on index cards: *gorilla, giraffe, zebra, bear, monkey, tiger, lion, elephant, alligator, panda, seal, hippo.* Write the following body parts on index cards and draw a simple picture next to each one: *ears, nose, eyes, tail, teeth, arms, legs, neck, mouth.* Write the adjectives on the board for students to use as a reference: *long, short, big, small.* Place the animal cards in one pile facedown. Place the body part cards in another pile facedown. Model the activity for students. Students take turns choosing one card from each pile. Students then say a sentence using each word. For example, if students choose *seal* and *neck,* their sentence might be: *A seal has a short neck.*

### My Favorite Animal

Show students a picture that you have cut out or drawn of your favorite animal. Label the picture and write one or two sentences about it. For example: *An elephant has big ears. An elephant has a long trunk.* Give each student a piece of drawing paper, and crayons or markers.

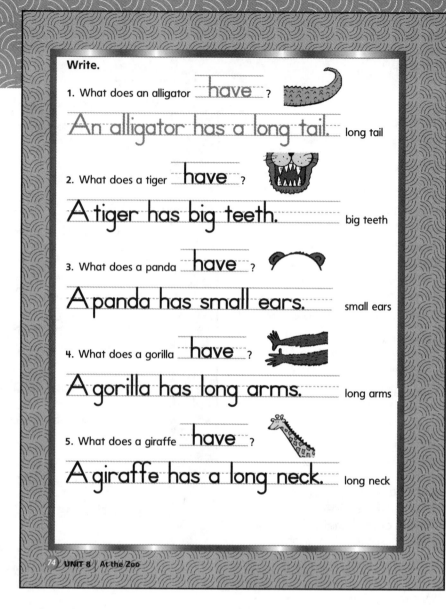

Write.

1. What does an alligator **have** ?
An alligator has a long tail.    long tail

2. What does a tiger **have** ?
A tiger has big teeth.    big teeth

3. What does a panda **have** ?
A panda has small ears.    small ears

4. What does a gorilla **have** ?
A gorilla has long arms.    long arms

5. What does a giraffe **have** ?
A giraffe has a long neck.    long neck

74    UNIT 8    At the Zoo

Students draw a picture of their favorite animal and then share it with the rest of the class. As students are talking about and describing their animal, encourage them to use language from this unit: *A (panda) has (small) (ears).*

### Guessing Game

Hold up each Picture Card and review the animal names with students. Place the Picture Cards facedown on the floor or on a table in front of students. Ask them to close their eyes. Take away one Picture Card. Ask students to open their eyes. Students then guess which card is missing. After they have guessed, ask them to describe the animal using language from this lesson: *A monkey has small hands.*

### Animal Masks

Bring in paper plates and craft sticks. Show students a completed mask you have made by decorating a paper plate. Describe the animal with language from this unit: *A panda has small ears.* Students work in groups while making their masks. Help students cut out the eyes. Help them fasten the craft stick to the bottom of the mask so they can hold it up to their faces. Invite each student to come and tell which animal they are and to describe it using language from this lesson: *This is a (seal). A seal has (short) (legs).*

**Vocabulary:** alligator, bear, big, elephant, giraffe, gorilla, hippo, lion, long, monkey, panda, seal, short, small, tiger, zebra

### Lesson Objectives
✓ to name zoo animals

✓ to use the possessives *its* and *theirs*

✓ to use singular and plural possessive nouns: *(lion's)* and *(lions')*

### Classroom English
• Find. Say. Color. Draw. Write. Show me. What is it? Whose (ears) are (big)?

### Language Patterns
• The alligator's tail is long. Its tail is long.

• The lions' teeth are big. Their teeth are big.

### Materials
• One set of Picture Cards for each student; four sets of Picture Cards for each group; poster board; numerals *0, 1, 2* written on index cards three times; tape

• **Picture Cards:** gorilla, giraffe, zebra, bear, monkey, tiger, lion, elephant, alligator, panda, seal, hippo

## Its/Their

The alligator's tail is long.　　The lions' teeth are big.

Its tail is long.　　Their teeth are big.

**Write.**

1. The elephants' ears are big.

   Their ears are big.

2. The monkey's arms are long.

   Its arms are long.

3. The giraffes' necks are long.

   Their necks are long.

4. The panda's ears are small.

   Its ears are small.

## WARMING UP

Show students the zoo animal picture cards and ask them to identify each one. Hold up the *alligator* and say: *The alligator's tail is long.* Write this sentence on the board and read it with students. Remind them that the *'s* shows possession. Write a new sentence next to it: *Its tail is long.* Underline the word *Its* and explain that the word *Its* replaces the word *alligator's* and shows possession. Point out the word *its* does not have an apostrophe. Repeat the activity using other animals.

Use multiple copies of Picture Cards for this activity. Show students two elephants and model the sentence: *The elephants' ears are big.* Read the sentence with students. Circle the *s'* and explain that this shows possession and that that there is more than one elephant. Explain that in cases like this, the apostrophe goes after the *s.* Now write a new sentence: *Their ears are big.* Explain that the word *their* replaces the word *elephants',* is plural, and shows possession. Repeat the activity using other animals from this unit.

## 🎧 USING PAGE 75

Help students find page 75 in their books. Ask students to identify the animals and to describe them. Play the recording or read the Grammar Box. Explain that *'s* is singular and shows possession, and that *s'* is plural and shows possession. Point out how the possessive *its* replaces the singular possessive noun and the possessive *their* replaces the plural possessive noun.

Read the directions for the activity and ask students to read with you. Read the first sentence and point out the possessive noun. Read the revised sentence and explain that the word *their* replaces the word *elephants'.* Ask students to trace the second sentence. Use a similar procedure to complete the page with students. Write the answers on the board so students can self-check their work.

## USING PAGE 76

Help students find page 76 in their books. Read the directions and ask students to read with you. Read the first sentence with students. Ask students to tell which animals have big teeth and then to draw a picture of one of them in the box. Students' answers will vary. Use a similar procedure to complete the page with students. When they are finished, invite them to tell which animals they drew.

## HAVING FUN!
### Information Gap Activity

Give each student a set of Picture Cards. Model the activity. Students sit back-to-back with their cards facedown in a pile. The first student turns over his or her card and then gives a clue. For example, if Student 1 turns over the Picture Card *giraffe,* he or she says: *Its neck is long.* Student 2 continues to guess until he or she guesses correctly: *It's a giraffe.* Students then switch roles and play again.

### A Card Game

Make four sets of Picture Cards for each group of students. Students play in groups of three or four. Model how the game is played. Deal out all the cards to each student. Show students how to hold their cards like a fan so no one can see which animals they have. Students begin by placing any pairs they have on the table. Students name each animal and describe it using language from this unit: *It is a (lion). Its (teeth) are (big).* The first student turns to the student on his or her left and chooses a card from that person's hand. If the card matches one in their hand, they place the pair down, name the animal, and describe it. Play continues clockwise around the circle. Students continue choosing a card from the student on their left

until all the matches are found. The student with the most pairs at the end of the game wins.

### A Board Game

Use the Picture Cards from this unit and a large piece of poster board to make a game board. Glue the Picture Cards in an *S* pattern on the game board. Label *Start* and *Finish*. Write the numerals 0, 1, 2 on index cards three times so there are nine cards. Place these facedown in the middle of the table or floor. Use small pieces of paper or paper clips for markers. Model how the game is played. Students take turns choosing one of the index cards and then moving their marker the correct number of spaces along the game board. The student

who reaches the finish line first wins. As students land on an animal, encourage them to name the animal and to describe it using language from this unit: *It is a (lion). Its teeth are big.*

### Sorting

Write the following sentences on the board as column headings: *Their teeth are big. Their tails are long. Their ears are small. Their ears are big. Their tails are short. Their mouths are big. Their mouths are small.* Show students each Picture Card and help them decide which column it belongs in and then tape it in place. After all the animals are sorted, ask students to identify them and to describe them using language from this unit.

---

**Draw.**

1. Its teeth are big.

(drawing will vary)

2. Its tail is long.

(drawing will vary)

3. Its ears are big.

(drawing will vary)

4. Its tail is short.

(drawing will vary)

5. Its mouth is big.

(drawing will vary)

**Vocabulary:** alligator, bear, elephant, giraffe, gorilla, hippo, lion, monkey, panda, seal, tiger, zebra

**Lesson Objectives**
✓ to identify zoo animals
✓ to describe animals using adjectives
✓ to use the possessives *its* and *theirs*

**Classroom English**
• Play. Show me. Find. Say. What is it?

**Language Patterns**
• Its (teeth) are (big).
• Its (mouth) is (big).

**Materials**
• **Picture Cards:** gorilla, giraffe, zebra, bear, monkey, tiger, lion, elephant, alligator, panda, seal, hippo

## WARMING UP

Begin by reviewing vocabulary from this unit. Show students the Picture Cards and ask them to identify the zoo animals. Model if necessary. Ask students to describe the animals using language from this unit: *It's a (hippo). Its (mouth) is (big).* Model if necessary.

## 🎧 USING PAGE 77

Help students find page 77 in their books. Play the recording or read the chant for students. Point to each Picture Card as the word appears in the chant. Model and ask students to follow along and point to each word as they listen. After they have listened to and read the chant a few times, invite students to say it with you. Encourage them to point to each word as they read. Place the corresponding Picture Cards on the board. Say the chant again and invite students to come up and point to the corresponding Picture Cards as they appear in the chant.

🎧 Chant.

Its teeth are big.
Its teeth are big.
It's a lion!
It's a lion!

Its ears are small.
Its ears are small.
It's a bear!
It's a bear!

Its arms are long.
Its arms are long.
It's a monkey!
It's a monkey!

Its mouth is big.
Its mouth is big.
It's a hippo!
It's a hippo!

Punctuation, *Have/Has, Its/Their* 77

## EXTENSION
### Continue the Chant

Review the chant with students by playing the recording or reading it for them. Substitute other zoo animals and descriptions. Students say the new chant. Invite volunteers to come up and point to the corresponding Picture Cards as they hear them in the chant.

### Act Out the Chant

Review the chant with students by playing the recording or reading it for them. Ask students to point to the corresponding body part and to act out what the animal does.

### Take the Parts

Divide the class into two groups.

Groups alternate saying the first two lines and the second two lines.

### It's and Its

Write the following sentences on the board and leave out the words indicated. Write the words *it's and its* on the board. Read each sentence with students and help them fill in the missing word. Explain that the word *its* indicates possession and the word *it's* is a contraction for *it is.*

1. _____ ears are big.
2. _____ an elephant.
3. _____ arms are long.
4. _____ a seal.
5. _____ an alligator.
6. _____ mouth is big.

When students are finished, ask them to add other sentences.

**Vocabulary:** alligator, bear, elephant, giraffe, gorilla, hippo, lion, monkey, panda, seal, tiger, zebra

**Lesson Objectives**

✓ to identify zoo animals

✓ to describe zoo animals

✓ to use the possessives *their* and *its*

**Classroom English**

• Play. Show me. Find. Say. Write. Color.

**Language Patterns**

• It's a (lion).

• Its (tail) is (long).

**Materials**

• Crayons and pencils or markers

• **Picture Cards:** gorilla, giraffe, zebra, bear, monkey, tiger, lion, elephant, alligator, panda, seal, hippo

## WARMING UP

Show students the Picture Cards for this unit and review the zoo animals with them. As you say each zoo animal name, write it on the board and read it with students. Invite students to use language from this lesson: *It's a (lion). Its mouth is big.*

## USING PAGE 78

Help students find page 78 in their books. Show them the picture. Read the words with students. Explain that the animals are hidden in the picture. Ask students to find and color each animal. When they are finished, invite them to sit with a partner, identify the animals, and describe them using language from this lesson.

## EXTENSION
### Hidden Animals

Hide the zoo animal Picture Cards around the room. Invite students to go on an animal safari. Students keep the Picture Cards they find. After all

### Find and color.

giraffe    elephant    hippo    alligator    gorilla    bear

the animals have been found, ask students to sit in a circle and to identify each animal. Students can also describe the animals using language from this unit: *It's a (bear). Its (tail) is (small).*

# Units 7 & 8

Review

**Vocabulary:** alligator, bear, bread, carrot, cheese, chicken, elephant, fish, giraffe, gorilla, hippo, lion, mango, monkey, onion, orange, panda, potato, rice, seal, soup, tiger, tomato, water, zebra

### Review Objectives

✓ to identify foods

✓ to identify zoo animals

✓ to identify singular, plural, and noncount nouns

✓ to identify the possessives *Its* and *Their*

✓ to identify simple present tense *have* and *has*

### Classroom English

• Listen. Check. Point. Say.

### Language Patterns

• I want (3) (carrots).

• Its (tail) is (long).

• Their (feet) are (big).

• A (panda) has (small) (ears).

### Materials

• **Realia:** foods, fruits, vegetables from this unit, toy zoo animals

• **Picture Cards:** chicken, soup, cheese, tomato, potato, carrot, onion, rice, bread, mango, orange, water, gorilla, giraffe, zebra, bear, monkey, tiger, lion, elephant, alligator, panda, seal, hippo

## WARMING UP

Review the zoo animals from Unit 7. Hold up toy animals or Picture Cards. Ask: *What is it?* Invite students to use a complete sentence when answering: *(It is/It's) a (zebra).*

## Review: Units 7 and 8

### Vocabulary
A. Listen and check.

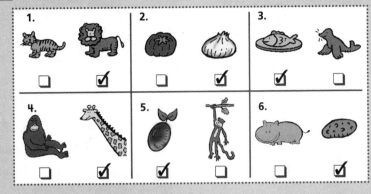

### Singular and Plural Nouns
B. Listen and check.

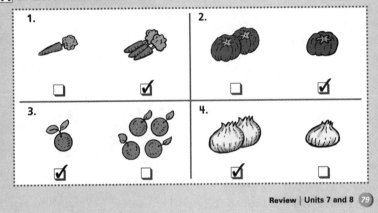

Review | Units 7 and 8  79

Review the food items with students. Begin with the countable items. Show one and more than one of each item. Ask: *What is it?* and *What are they?* Students should respond: *It's a (tomato). They are (tomatoes).*

Review the noncount food items with students. Remind them that we can't count these items and that we don't use the words *a* or *an* before noncount nouns. Ask: *What is it?* and model the response: *It's (cheese).*

Show students the Picture Cards for the zoo animals. Ask them to describe the animals. For example: *It's (tail) is (long). Their (feet) are (big).* Model sentences and then ask students to say sentences of their own.

Repeat the previous procedure and model sentences that use *have* and *has.* For example: *The (giraffe) has a (long) (neck).*

---

### AUDIOSCRIPT

**A.** 1. lion    2. onion    3. fish    4. giraffe    5. mango    6. potato

**B.** 1. I want three carrots.    2. I want a tomato.    3. I want an orange.    4. I want two onions.

Tape two animal Picture Cards to the board and draw a small box under each one. Say: *It's a (giraffe)*. Point to the Picture Cards and ask students to tell which card goes with your sentence. Invite a student to place a check in the correct box.

Tape one animal Picture Card to the board. Write *yes* and *no* under the Picture Card and draw a box next to each word. Say a sentence: *It is a (giraffe)*. Students should verify if the sentence you said is correct or incorrect according to the picture.

If you feel students need to practice exercises that are similar to those presented in the Review Units, use exercises like the one above so students can practice checking boxes and pictures that go with stated sentences are words. You can use similar exercises for any of the Review Exercises at the end of the unit.

## USING PAGE 79

Help students find page 79 in their books. Help students find Exercise A. Read the directions and ask students to follow along. Point to each picture and ask students to say the words with you. Explain to students that they should check the picture that goes with the word they hear. Play the recording or read the audioscript for students. Students check the correct picture.

Help students find Exercise B. Read the directions and ask students to follow along. Point to the picture and ask students to repeat each word after you. Ask students to tell how many they see of each food. Explain to students that they should check

## Review: Units 7 and 8

### Its/Their
🎧 **C. Listen and check.**

### Have/Has
🎧 **D. Listen, point, and say.**

80 Review | Units 7 and 8

the picture that goes with the sentence they hear. Play the recording or read the audioscript. Students check the correct picture.

## USING PAGE 80

Help students find page 80 in their books. Help students find Exercise C. Read the directions and ask students to follow along. Point to the pictures and ask students to describe the different animal body parts and to

use the possessives *its* and *their*. For example: *Its (tail) is (long)*. Explain to students that they should check the *yes* box if the sentence they hear matches the picture. They should check the *no* box if the sentence does not match the picture.

Help students find Exercise D. Read the directions and ask students to follow along. Explain that they should listen, point to the picture, and then say the sentence. Play the recording or read the audioscript for students.

---

### AUDIOSCRIPT

**C.** 1. Its tail is short.    2. Their teeth are big.    3. Its neck is long.
    4. Their arms are long.    5. Their ears are small.    6. Its ears are big.

**D.** 1. An alligator has a long tail.    2. Lions have big teeth.    3. A panda has small ears.
    4. Gorillas have long arms.    5. A hippo has short legs.    6. Giraffes have long necks.

# Unit 9
## Celebrations

### Always/Never, Sometimes, When...?

**Vocabulary:** dance in a parade, give presents, make a wish, send cards, visit family or friends, watch fireworks, wear a mask

---

#### Lesson Objectives
✓ to identify celebrations
✓ to use the adverb of frequency *always*

#### Classroom English
• Find. Say. Circle. Color. Draw. Write. Show me. What is it? It is a (card). What do you do? I (dance).

#### Language Pattern
• I always wear a (mask).

#### Materials
• Crayons; markers; drawing paper; bag or box; slips of paper with words: *visit, wear, send, dance, watch, make a wish, give;* paper plates; craft sticks; old calendar pages
• **Picture Cards:** dance in a parade, give presents, make a wish, send cards, visit family or friends, watch fireworks, wear a mask

---

### Celebrations

visit family

give presents

wear a mask

send cards

dance in a parade

watch fireworks

make a wish

*Always/Never, Sometimes, When...?* 81

### WARMING UP

Show students the following Picture Cards: *watch fireworks, make a wish, dance in a parade, send cards, give presents, wear a mask, visit family or friends.* Introduce one Picture Card at a time. Ask students to repeat the phrases after you say each one. Place the Picture Cards on the board and ask students to point to pictures as you say the phrases: *Find (watch fireworks).* Encourage students to say: *I (watch fireworks).*

Ask students to tell when they do each activity. Have ready three pages from an old calendar to illustrate the meaning of *always, sometimes,* and *never.* Display a calendar page with every date checked, shaded, or otherwise filled in to show the meaning of *always;* a calendar page

with half of the dates filled in to show the meaning of *sometimes;* and a calendar page with none of the dates filled in to show the meaning of *never.* You may want to recycle vocabulary from previous units as appropriate: *I always (eat breakfast). I sometimes (fly a kite). I never (play with a yo-yo).* Encourage students to use both recycled and new vocabulary in complete sentences.

### 🎧 USING PAGE 81

Help students find page 81 in their books. Play the recording or read the words. Allow students to talk about the pictures and encourage them to identify the actions. Explain that people do special things on holidays.

As you say each new phrase, point to the corresponding picture and ask students to repeat.

Allow students to describe how they celebrate a holiday in their homes. You may want to make a list of words that students will need for their descriptions on the board.

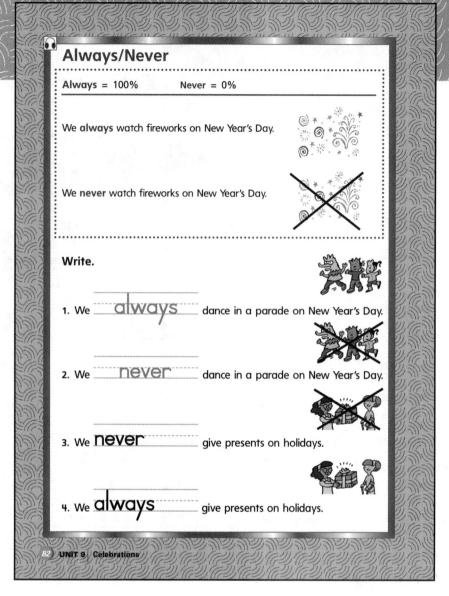

## Always/Never

Always = 100%          Never = 0%

We **always** watch fireworks on New Year's Day.

We **never** watch fireworks on New Year's Day.

**Write.**

1. We __always__ dance in a parade on New Year's Day.

2. We __never__ dance in a parade on New Year's Day.

3. We **never** give presents on holidays.

4. We **always** give presents on holidays.

82  UNIT 9  Celebrations

---

## USING PAGE 82

Help students find page 82 in their books. Draw their attention to the word *Always* at the top of the page. Display the calendar pages illustrating the meaning of *always, sometimes,* and *never* used in the warm-up activity on page 81. Ask students to identify which calendar page shows the meaning of *always.* Play the recording or read the Grammar Box and ask students to read with you. Explain that the adverb *always* means 100 percent, or all of the time. Repeat the same procedure for *never.* Point out that the cross (**X**) over the fireworks indicates something we do not do.

Allow students to talk about the picture and to tell what they always and never do on holidays. Ask volunteers to first read the sentences and then tell what they do.

Read the directions for the activity and ask students to read with you. Ask students to identify the activities in the pictures and to tell how often they do them. Tell students that they will be using the adverbs *always* and *never* to complete the sentences. Remind students that an **X** means *never.* Read the first sentence with students. Explain that the correct answer is *always* (there is no **X** over the activity). Ask students to trace the word *always* to complete the sentence. Use a similar procedure to complete the page with students. Write the answers on the board so students can self-check their work.

## HAVING FUN!
### Act It Out

Write the following actions on slips of paper: *visit friends, wear a mask, send cards, dance in a parade, watch fireworks, make a wish, give presents.* Place the corresponding Picture Cards on the board. Read each one with

students. Fold the slips of paper and place them in a box or bag. Model the activity. Students take turns choosing a slip of paper and then acting out the phrase. The student who guesses correctly points to the corresponding Picture Card, and then becomes the next actor.

### Picture Card Sort

Place the following Picture Cards on the board or on the floor in front of students: *cut, draw* (from Unit One), *seesaw, swing* (from Unit Two), *computer, radio, bike, telephone* (from Unit Three), *library, supermarket, post office, bookstore* (from Unit Four), *get dressed, play the piano, listen to music* (Unit Five), *water,*

*orange, bread, cheese, soup, rice, chicken* (from Unit Six), *visit family or friends, wear a mask, give presents, send cards, dance in a parade, watch fireworks, make a wish* (from this unit). Explain to students that they will choose pictures that represent activities they always do. Model the activity. Pick up a Picture Card *(rice)* and say: *I always (eat rice).* Put the Picture Card in a separate pile, one reserved for activities students <u>always</u> do. Invite students to go through the Picture Cards, choose those that represent actions they always do, make sentences, and put the Picture Cards in the pile reserved for activities they always do.

**Vocabulary:** dance in a parade, give presents, make a wish, send cards, visit family or friends, watch fireworks, wear a mask

### Lesson Objectives
✓ to identify celebrations

✓ to use the adverbs of frequency *always, never, sometimes*

✓ to tell when we do an activity

### Classroom English
• Find. Say. Color. Draw. Write. Show me. What is it? It is a (card). What do you do? I (dance).

### Language Pattern
• I (always/never/sometimes) dance in a parade on New Year's Day.

### Materials
• Markers; crayons; drawing paper; large poster board; words on index cards: *visit, wear, send, dance, watch, fireworks, parade, mask, make a wish, friend, family, card, give, present*

• **Picture Cards:** dance in a parade, give presents, make a wish, send cards, visit family or friends, watch fireworks, wear a mask

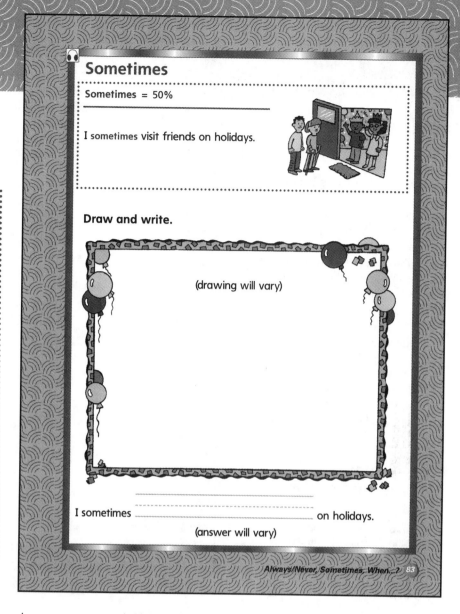

## Sometimes

Sometimes = 50%

I sometimes visit friends on holidays.

**Draw and write.**

(drawing will vary)

I sometimes  on holidays.

(answer will vary)

## WARMING UP

Show students the Picture Cards from this unit and ask students to identify each activity. Display the calendar pages illustrating the meaning of *always, sometimes,* and *never* used in the warm-up activity on page 81.

Hold up one of the Picture Cards and ask students if they do the activity. Help them reply using language they know or language from this lesson. Model the sentence. For example, if a student points to the calendar page illustrating *never* and you are holding up the Picture Card: *dance in a parade,* model a sentence such as: *I never dance in a parade on New Year's Day.* Ask the student and the rest of the class to repeat. Continue the activity with other students. Write

these sentences on the board for students to read with you.

## 🎧 USING PAGE 83

Help students find page 83 in their books. Draw their attention to the word *Sometimes* at the top of the page. Display the calendar pages illustrating the meaning of *always, never,* and *sometimes* used in the warm-up activity on page 81 to check for understanding. Play the recording or read the Grammar Box and ask students to read with you. Explain that the adverb *sometimes* means 50 percent, or some of the time.

Read the directions for the activity and ask students to read with you. Show students a completed picture

you have drawn ahead of time. Allow them to talk about the picture and to tell what you sometimes do on holidays. Ask students to draw a picture showing what they sometimes do on holidays and then to write the corresponding verb on the line. When they are finished, invite students to share their pictures and to read to the class.

## Using Page 84

Help students find page 84 in their books. Read the directions for the activity and ask students to read with you. Draw their attention to the illustrations and ask students to identify the activities. Explain that students will make true sentences about themselves by writing the word that best describes their real holiday behavior. For example, if a student always gives presents on a certain holiday, he or she would circle *always* and then write *always* on the line. Look at the first sentence with students and help them complete it according to their own habits. Use a similar procedure to complete the page with students.

## Having Fun!
### Listening Game in Teams

Place the Picture Cards on the board. Divide the class into two teams. Ask each team to make a line from the front to the back of the room. Model how the game is played. Whisper a sentence from this lesson to the first student in each line. Ask students to wait until you say *Go!* After you give the signal, students whisper the sentence as fast as they can to the next student in line, and continue whispering until the last student is reached. The last student says the sentence and points to the corresponding Picture Card. The team that completes this first is the winner. While students are playing, change their places in line so they get to be either the first or last student in line.

### An Activity Game

Draw a large circle on a piece of poster board and divide the circle into seven pie-shaped spaces. Place a mark in the center of the circle. Glue the Picture Cards in the spaces. Use a pencil as a spinner. Show students how to play the game. Students take turns spinning the pencil, identifying the activity, and then saying a sentence. For example, if the spinner points to *dance in a parade*, students can say: *I (sometimes) (dance in a parade) on (New Year's Day)*.

### Matching

Write the following phrases on index cards and read them with students: *visit family or friends, wear a mask, send cards, dance in a parade, watch fireworks, make a wish, give presents*. Place these facedown on one side of a table or on the floor in front of students. Show students the Picture Cards from this unit and ask them to identify the actions. Place these face down on the other side of the table or floor. Model how the game is played. Students take turns turning over one index card and one Picture Card. If they find a match, they keep the pair. Continue playing until all the pairs have been found. The student with the most pairs at the end of the game wins. Encourage students to use each word in a sentence that uses language from this lesson.

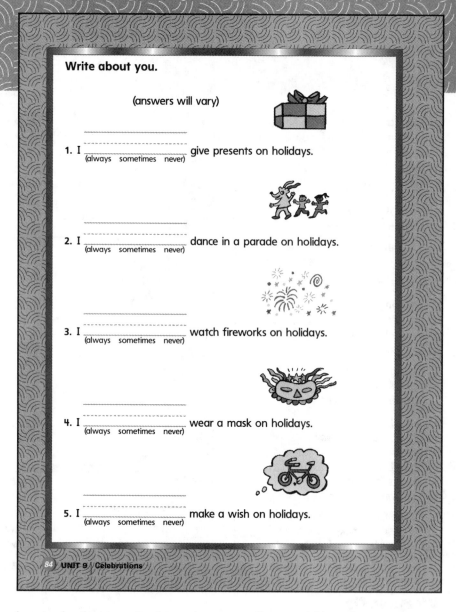

**Write about you.**

(answers will vary)

1. I _____ give presents on holidays.
   (always   sometimes   never)

2. I _____ dance in a parade on holidays.
   (always   sometimes   never)

3. I _____ watch fireworks on holidays.
   (always   sometimes   never)

4. I _____ wear a mask on holidays.
   (always   sometimes   never)

5. I _____ make a wish on holidays.
   (always   sometimes   never)

84   UNIT 9   Celebrations

**Vocabulary:** dance in a parade, give presents, make a wish, send cards, visit family or friends, watch fireworks, wear a mask

### Lesson Objectives
✓ to ask questions using the question word *when*

✓ to identify and use the months of the year

✓ to talk about celebrations

### Classroom English
• Find. Say. Color. Draw. Write. Show me. What month is it?

### Language Patterns
• When is (her) birthday?

• (Her) birthday is in (December).

### Materials
• The months of the year on two sets of index cards, poster board, twelve-month calendar, blank yearly calendar for each student, large piece of brown paper, game pieces

## WARMING UP

Show students a calendar that has the twelve months of the year. Say each month as you point to it and ask students to say the months with you.

Draw a cake with birthday candles on the board and say: *My birthday is in (May).* Invite each student to come up and point to the month of his or her birthday. Assist students as necessary. Model a sentence for each student and ask the students to say it with you. For example, if a student points to July, model the sentence: *My birthday is in July.* Write each of the sentences on the board and help each student read his or her sentence.

Play a memory game with students. Ask individual students to tell when their classmates' birthdays are. Assist as necessary and model sentences such as: *(Sally's/Bill's) birthday is in*

June. (Her/His) birthday is in (June). Write the sentences on the board and read them with students.

Model the question: *When is your birthday?* and ask students to say it with you a few times. Ask each student this question and help them answer using language from this lesson. Invite students to ask each other: *When is your birthday?* and to respond: *My birthday is in (September).*

## 🎧 USING PAGE 85

Help students find page 85 in their books. Ask students to talk about the picture and to identify the months in the calendars in the box. Play the recording or read the Grammar Box. Explain that we use the question

word *when* when we want to know the time an activity happens.

Read the directions for the activity and ask students to read with you. Ask students to identify the months pictured. Explain that they will be writing a question and filling in the month for each picture. Read the word in parentheses in number 1 with students. Point to the calendar that shows the word *December.* Read the question and answer for number 1. Ask students to trace the words for the question and to trace the word *December* to complete the response. Use a similar procedure to complete the page with students. Write the answers on the board so students can self-check their work.

## USING PAGE 86

Help students find page 86 in their books. Read the directions and ask students to read with you. Point to each month of the year and ask students to repeat the name after you. Explain that students will be circling the months for their fathers' birthdays, their own birthdays, and other family members' and friends' birthdays. Students can write about five family members and friends and tell when their birthdays are. You may want to make a list of words on the board: *mother, grandmother, grandfather, aunt, uncle, brother, sister, cousin.* Circulate as students are working to provide assistance.

## HAVING FUN!
### Which Month Is Missing?

Write the months of the year on the board at random for students and ask them to read the months with you. Ask students to close their eyes. Erase one of the months. Students open their eyes and guess which month is missing. Students score one point for each correct answer. Students can score an additional point if they can use the month in a sentence about a family member such as: *My father's birthday is in October.* The student with the most points at the end of the game wins.

### The Months in Order

Write the months of the year on two sets of index cards and read them with students. Then shuffle the cards in each set and place them in a pile facedown on the table or floor. Model how the game is played, and practice a few times with students before playing. Invite two students to come up and place their set of index cards in the correct order so the months are arranged from *January* to *December.* The student who does this first wins.

### Information Gap Activity

Show students a calendar you have made that has the twelve months of the year on it. Write the months of the year on the board for students to use as a reference. Give each student a blank twelve month calendar and ask them to write the months, in order, on their calendars. Model the activity. Students use their calendars and a marker to play. Students sit back-to-back. Student 1 places his or her marker on one of the months. Student 2 guesses which month it is by saying one of the months. Student 2 continues to guess until he or she guesses correctly. Students then switch roles and play again.

### Months of the Year Hopscotch

Make a hopscotch board on a large sheet of brown paper or play outside. You should have two columns of six spaces. Write one month in each space, following the order from *January* to *December.* Show students how to play. Students take turns tossing a marker such as a pebble onto the first month, *January.* Students say each month as they hop from square to square. Students continue playing by tossing the pebble on the next month until they reach *December.* The student who reaches *December* first wins.

---

**Circle and write.**

### My Family and Friends

| January | February | March | April | May | June |
|---|---|---|---|---|---|

| July | August | September | October | November | December |
|---|---|---|---|---|---|

(answers will vary)

1. My father's birthday is in _____ .

2. My _____ .

3. _____

4. _____

5. _____

**Vocabulary:** dance in a parade, give presents, make a wish, send cards, visit family or friends, watch fireworks, wear a mask

### Lesson Objectives
✓ to talk about celebrations
✓ to use the frequency adverbs *always, sometimes, never*

### Classroom English
• Show me. Find. Say. What is it? What do you do?

### Language Patterns
• I (never/always/sometimes) (wear) a (mask) on (New Year's Day).

### Marterials
• blank calendars, hole punch, string
• **Realia:** card, present, mask
• **Picture Cards:** dance in a parade, give presents, make a wish, send cards, visit family or friends, watch fireworks, wear a mask

## WARMING UP

Review the vocabulary from this unit by showing students the Picture Cards and asking them to identify the words. Ask students to tell when they do these activities by using the frequency adverbs *always, sometimes, never.*

##  USING PAGE 87

Help students find page 87 in their books. Play the recording or read the chant for students. Point to each month on a calendar as the word appears in the chant. Model and ask students to read with you and point to each word as they listen. After they have listened to and read the chant a few times, invite students to say it with you. Encourage them to point to each word as they read. Place the corresponding calendar pages on the board. Say the chant again and invite students to come up and point to the

🎧 **Chant.**

When is your birthday?
When is your birthday?
My birthday is in May.
My birthday is in May.

January, February, March,
April, May, June,
July, August, September,
October, November, December.

*Always/Never, Sometimes, When...?* **87**

corresponding months as they hear them in the chant.

## EXTENSION
### Continue the Chant

Review the chant with students by playing the recording or reading it for them. Substitute *your birthday* in the question with a student's name: *When is (Bill's) birthday? When is (Mary's) birthday?* Adjust answers as necessary: *(His/her) birthday is in (June).* Model if necessary.

### A Month of Celebrations

Give each student a blank monthly calendar and ask them to write the month it currently is at the top. Help

students write the numerals for each day. Go through the days of the current month with students and ask them to tell you which celebrations they observe and to find the corresponding day on their calendar. Write the names for each celebration mentioned on the board and ask students to fill in any celebrations that pertain to them. You may want to do more than one month.

**Vocabulary:** months of the year, give presents

## WARMING UP

Show students the Picture Cards for this unit and review the celebrations with them. Point to the *give presents* Picture Card and ask students to identify it. Draw a simple maze on the board ahead of time and place the *give presents* Picture Card at the end. Invite students to find the Picture Card by completing the maze with you.

## USING PAGE 88

Help students find page 88 in their books. Read the directions and ask students to read with you. Ask students to point to the present at the end of the maze and then model how to complete the maze by tracing the path with your finger. As you do this, say each month of the year as you pass it in the maze. Ask students to say the months with you. Explain that the path follows the months as they happen in order during the year. Students complete the maze with a partner.

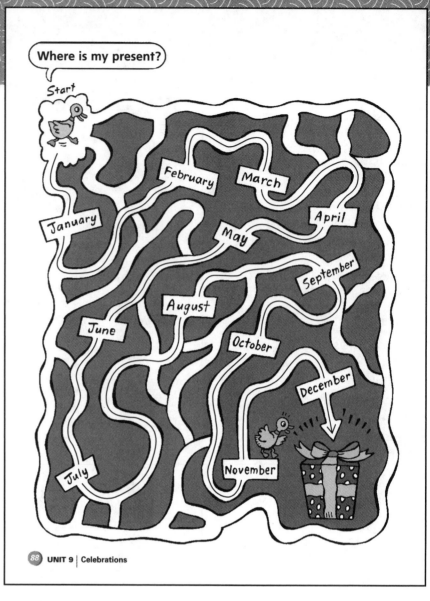

## EXTENSION
### A Hunt

Use Picture Cards from this unit. Place them around the class ahead of time. You will have seven items for students to find. Write each vocabulary phrase on a slip of paper. Read each one with students and then place them in a bag or box. Determine if students should hunt alone, in groups, or in pairs, so all seven items will be found and so that each student participates. Model the activity. Students pick a slip of paper, read it, and then hunt for that item. Encourage them to ask: *Where is (send cards)?* When everyone has found their Picture Card, invite students to sit in a circle and to tell what they found.

# Unit 10
## Transportation

### How...?

**Vocabulary:** airplane, bike, boat, bus, car, helicopter, motorcycle, subway, taxi, train

---

#### Lesson Objectives
✓ to identify vehicles

✓ to talk about different types of transportation

✓ to ask and answer questions with *how, I,* and *you*

✓ to use the preposition *by* to tell how we get from place to place

#### Classroom English
• Find. Say. Circle. Color. Draw. Write. Show me. What is it? It is a (car).

#### Language Patterns
• How do you go to (school)?

• I go to (school) by (car).

#### Materials
• Crayons, markers, drawing paper, scissors, old magazines, newspapers, glue, large poster board or large piece of construction paper, box or bag, vehicle names on slips of paper, one set of Picture Cards for each pair of students

• **Picture Cards:** car, bus, subway, airplane, helicopter, bike, taxi, motorcycle

---

### WARMING UP

Show students the following Picture Cards: *car, bus, subway, airplane, helicopter, bike, taxi, motorcycle.* Introduce one Picture Card at a time. Ask students to repeat the new words after you say each one. After students are familiar with the vocabulary, ask: *What is it?* Model the response and ask students to repeat: *It is a (car). It is an (airplane).* Place the Picture Cards on the board or on the floor in front of students. Ask students to point to pictures as you name them: *Find the (bus).* After they have pointed to the picture encourage students to say: *It is a (bus).* Explain that a subway is a train

that runs underground in man-made tunnels.

Draw a simple picture of a school on the board and ask: *How do you go to school?* Hold up the *bus* Picture Card and ask students to stand if they go to school by bus. Model the sentence: *I go to school by bus.* Ask students to repeat. Use a similar procedure to help students talk about how they go to school. Hold up each Picture Card, ask students to stand, and model the response for students to repeat.

### 🎧 USING PAGE 89

Help students find page 89 in their books. Play the recording or read the words. Allow students to talk about

the pictures and encourage them to identify the words. Do a Show Me activity. Say sentences such as: *Show me a (bus). Show me a (taxi).* Students point to the picture and say the words with you. Model complete sentences as students point to and say each new vocabulary word: *It is a car.*

Help students find page 90 in their books. Ask students to identify the car and to tell what is happening in the picture: *A man is driving his car.* Play the recording or read the Grammar Box and ask students to read with you. Explain that we use the question word *how* when we want to know the way something is done.

Read the directions for the activity and ask students to read with you. Ask students to identify the vehicles. For number 1, read the question and response. Read the word in parentheses *(bus)*. Ask students to trace the word *How* to complete the question and trace the words to complete the response. Explain that the response uses the word in parentheses: *bus.* Use a similar procedure to complete the page with students. Write the answers on the board so students can self-check their work.

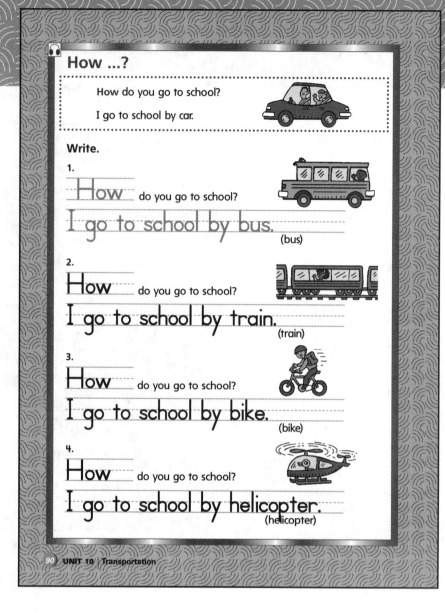

## HAVING FUN!
### A Transportation Collage

Prepare a model collage of transportation pictures ahead of time. Bring in old magazines and newspapers for students to cut up when making collages. Show students a collage you have made, ask them to identify each vehicle, and to talk about what is happening in the collage. Divide the students into groups and give each group a large piece of poster board or construction paper. Students cut out or draw transportation pictures and glue them to make a collage. When students are finished, ask them to present their collages. Students can take turns naming items and pointing to the corresponding pictures.

### Drawing Dictation

Model the activity. Give each student a piece of drawing paper and show them how to fold it into eight spaces. Students can draw eight pictures on the front and two pictures on the back. Give the following directions:

1. *Draw a red car.*
2. *Draw an orange bus.*
3. *Draw a yellow train.*
4. *Draw a green subway.*
5. *Draw a blue motorcycle.*
6. *Draw a purple airplane.*
7. *Draw a brown helicopter.*
8. *Draw a blue bike.*
9. *Draw a red boat.*
10. *Draw an orange taxi.*

When students are finished, ask them to label each picture and to share their work with a friend. Write the words on the board for students to use as a reference when labeling their pictures.

### Matching

Tape the Picture Cards in one column on the board. Write the transportation words in a second column, but in a different order so that students will have to match the word to the picture. Ask students to identify the pictures and help them read each word. Invite individual students to come up and draw a line from the word to the picture.

**Vocabulary:** airplane, bike, boat, bus, car, helicopter, motorcycle, subway, taxi, train

## WARMING UP

Show students the transportation Picture Cards and practice saying each word with them. After they have practiced each word, model a complete sentence and ask students to repeat: *It is a (car).* Give each student a piece of drawing paper and ask them to draw a picture showing how they go to school. You may want to write *on foot* on the board if students walk to school. When they are finished, invite a student to join you. Ask this student to show his or her picture to the class and ask: *How does (he/she) go to school?* Model the response and ask students to repeat: *(He/She) goes to school by (bike).* Continue in this manner, allowing each student to participate. Write the responses on the board and read them with students. Point out

that when we use *he/she* in a question, we use the helping word *does.* When we answer, the action word changes from *go* to *goes.*

## USING PAGE 91

Help students find page 91 in their books. Ask students to identify the train. Play the recording or read the Grammar Box and ask students to read with you. Explain that when we ask how *he* or *she* gets to work, we use the helping verb *does* in the question.

Read the directions for the activity and ask students to read with you. Ask students to identify the vehicle and to tell what is happening in each picture. Read the first question and

the word in parentheses: *bus.* Read the response and explain that the response uses the word in parentheses. Ask students to trace the word *How* to complete the question, and to trace each word to write the response. Use a similar procedure to complete the page with students. Write the answers on the board so students can self-check their work.

## Using Page 92

Help students find page 92 in their books. Read the directions for the activity and ask students to read with you. Ask students to talk about each picture and to identify the vehicles. Explain that each question and answer is about the picture to the right. Read the first question and answer with students and ask them to trace the word *How* to complete the question and to trace the words *by bike* to complete the response. Point out that these questions use the helping word *does* and that the verb *go* has a final *-es: goes.* Complete numbers 2 and 3 with students. Write the answers on the board so students can self-check their work.

Use a similar procedure to complete numbers 4–6. Point out that these questions use the helping word *does* and that the verb *go* has a final *-es: goes.* Write the answers on the board so students can self-check their work.

## Having Fun!
### Listening Game

Place the Picture Cards on the board and draw a simple picture of a boy and a girl. Label the girl *she* and the boy *he.* Ask students to form a line from the front to the back of the room. Whisper the sentence: *(He) (goes) to (work) by (bus).* to the first student in line. Motion for this student to whisper the sentence to the next student and so on, down the line. After the last student has heard the sentence, he or she says it out loud for everyone to hear. He or she then points to the correct Picture Card and the boy or girl on the board. The first student verifies if the sentence is correct. As students are playing, change their places in line so they get to be either the first or last student. You may want to form more than one

line so that more students participate at one time.

### Making New Sentences

Write the words *He, She,* and *I* on index cards three times each so you have nine cards. Cut out the Picture Cards from this unit so they can be used as playing cards. Place the Picture Cards facedown in a pile and the index cards facedown in a second pile. Model the activity for students. Students pick one card from each pile and make a sentence. For example, if students pick *He* and the Picture Card *car,* they say the sentence: *He goes to work by car.* After each student has played, ask them to return their Picture Card and index card to the bottom of the pile.

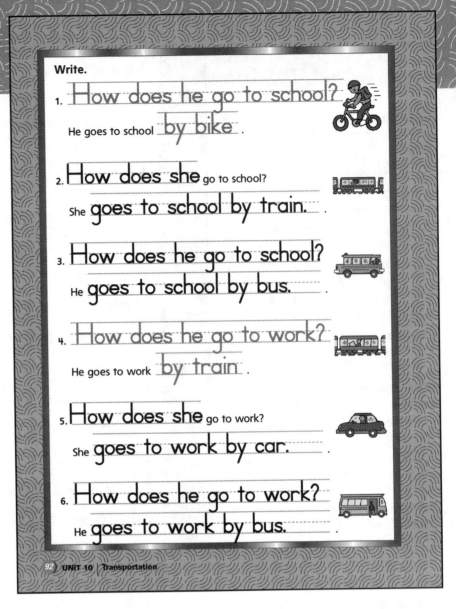

**Write.**

1. How does he go to school?
   He goes to school by bike.

2. How does she go to school?
   She goes to school by train.

3. How does he go to school?
   He goes to school by bus.

4. How does he go to work?
   He goes to work by train.

5. How does she go to work?
   She goes to work by car.

6. How does he go to work?
   He goes to work by bus.

92 UNIT 10 Transportation

**Vocabulary:** happy, hungry, sad, thirsty, tired

### Lesson Objectives
✓ to ask questions with the question word *how* to see how someone feels
✓ to use adjectives to describe how one feels

### Classroom English
• Find. Say. Color. Draw. Write. Show me.

### Language Patterns
• How are you feeling?
• I'm (happy).

### Materials
• Construction paper; markers; crayons; hole punch; string; pictures representing: *happy, sad, hungry, thirsty, tired* for each student

## WARMING UP

Show students pictures that represent the adjectives *happy, sad, hungry, thirsty, tired*. Model each one and ask students to repeat the words with you. Ask students: *How are you feeling?* Hold up the *happy* picture and model the response: *I'm happy.* Continue in this manner, asking students to practice questions and responses with the other adjectives: *sad, hungry, thirsty,* and *tired*.

## 🎧 USING PAGE 93

Help students find page 93 in their books. Play the recording or read the Grammar Box and ask students to read with you. Explain that we can ask about a person's condition or state by asking: *How are you feeling?* The response includes an adjective such as: *happy, sad, hungry, thirsty,* or *tired*.

Read the directions for the activity and ask students to read with you. Ask students to tell how each person feels as you point to each picture. Model if necessary. Read the question

and help students form the response: *I'm happy.* Write all the possible responses on the board for students to use as a reference when completing the first response. Use a similar procedure to complete the page. Write the sentences on the board so that students can self-check their work.

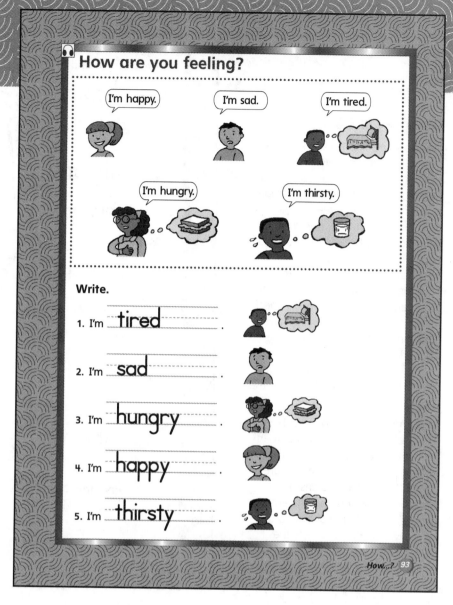

## USING PAGE 94

Help students find page 94 in their books. Read the directions for Exercise A and ask students to read with you. Read the letters in number 1 and help students see that when they are unscrambled, they form the word *happy.* Ask students to trace the word *happy.* Help students unscramble and write the words in numbers 2–4. Write the answers on the board so students can self-check their work. After all the words have been unscrambled, show students the circled word *happy* in the snake puzzle. Ask students to find the other words: *sad, thirsty,* and *hungry* in the snake puzzle.

Read the directions for items 1–3 of Exercise B and ask students to read with you. Ask students to identify the feelings represented in the pictures. Read the question and answer in number 1. Point out that the answer, *I'm sad,* matches the picture to the right. Invite students to trace the question and answer. Tell students to write an answer for items 2 and 3, using the pictures as clues. Read the directions for item 4 and ask students to read with you. Tell them to draw a face representing an emotion in the circle and then write a sentence describing that emotion. Write the answers for items 2 and 3 on the board for students so they can self-check their work. Invite students to show their drawings and read their sentences to the class.

## HAVING FUN!
### Ask and Answer

Students work in pairs. Give each pair of students pictures representing: *happy, sad, hungry, thirsty, cold, hot, tired.* Students place these pictures facedown in a pile. Student 1 asks: *How are you feeling?* Student 2 takes the top picture and responds using the word pictured: *I'm (sad).*

A. Unscramble and circle.

1. pyaph  happy

2. dsa  sad

3. yhitsrt  thirsty

4. nhgyur  hungry

B. Write.

1. How are you feeling?
   I'm sad.

2. I'm tired.

3. I'm thirsty.

C. Write and draw. (answer will vary)
   I'm

94  UNIT 10  Transportation

Students continue playing until all the pictures have been used. Students then switch roles and play again.

### *How are you feeling?* Books

Show students a completed book you have prepared ahead of time. Your book should have pictures that show: *happy, sad, hungry, thirsty, cold, hot,* and *tired.* Label each picture with a sentence: *I'm (hungry).* Make a cover with the question *How are you feeling?* on it, and a face showing one of the feelings. Encourage students to talk about your cover. Give each student three pieces of construction paper or drawing paper and show them how to fold them in half so they have six pages. Use a hole punch and string to assemble students' books. Students make a cover for their books, writing the question and drawing a picture. On the pages, students draw a face and write a matching sentence, for example, a happy face and *I'm happy.* Write the adjectives: *happy, sad, hungry, thirsty, cold, hot,* and *tired* on the board for students to use as a reference when working. Help students with spelling if necessary. When students are finished, invite them to show their books to the class and to talk about their pictures. Encourage them to use language from this unit such as: *I'm (hungry).*

**Vocabulary:** airplane, bike, boat, bus, car, helicopter, motorcycle, subway, taxi, train

**Lesson Objectives**
✓ to identify vehicles
✓ to tell how one goes to school

**Classroom English**
• Show me. Find. Say. What is it? It is a (train).

**Language Patterns**
• How do you go to school?
• I go to school by (bus).

**Materials**
• **Picture Cards:** car, bus, subway, airplane, helicopter, bike, taxi, motorcycle

## WARMING UP

Review vocabulary from this unit by showing students the transportation Picture Cards and asking them to identify the vehicles. Model if necessary. Place the Picture Cards on the board or on the floor in front of students. Ask: *How do you go to school?* Invite students to respond and point to the corresponding Picture Card. For example: *I go to school by (car).* Model if necessary.

##  USING PAGE 95

Help students find page 95 in their books. Play the recording or read the chant for students. Point to each Picture Card as the word appears in the chant. Model and ask students to read with you and point to each word as they listen. After they have listened to and read the chant a few times, invite them to say it with you. Encourage students to point to each word as they read. Place the corresponding Picture Cards on the board. Say the chant again and invite students to come up and point to the corresponding Picture Cards as they hear them in the chant.

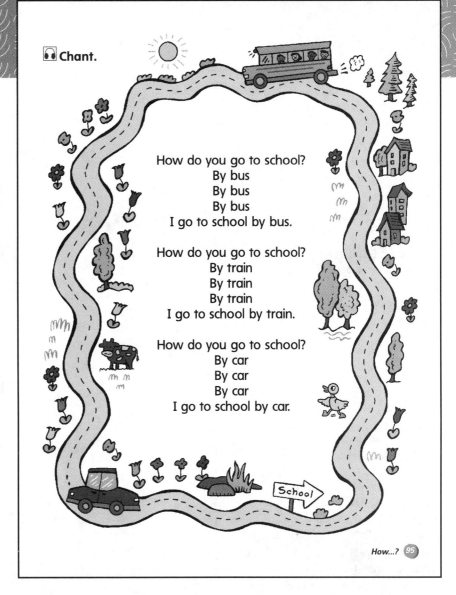

🎧 Chant.

How do you go to school?
By bus
By bus
By bus
I go to school by bus.

How do you go to school?
By train
By train
By train
I go to school by train.

How do you go to school?
By car
By car
By car
I go to school by car.

*How...?* 95

## EXTENSION
### Continue the Chant 1

Review the chant with students by playing the recording or reading it for them. Substitute other vehicles. Hold up new vehicle Picture Cards to prompt students as they say new verses. Model if necessary. You may want to include the expression *on foot* in the chant, using the Picture Card of a foot from Unit 1.

### Continue the Chant 2

Review the chant with students by playing the recording or reading it for them. Substitute *home* or *work* for *school* and say the chant again. Point to corresponding vehicle Picture Cards as you say the new chant. You may want to include the expression *on foot* in the chant, using the Picture Card of a foot from Unit 1.

### Act Out the Chant

Review the chant with students by playing the recording or reading it for them. Ask students to imitate each vehicle as they say it in the chant.

### Take the Parts

Divide the class into two groups. Groups take turns asking and answering the questions in the chant.

**Vocabulary:** airplane, bike, boat, bus, car, helicopter, motorcycle, subway, taxi, train

---

**Lesson Objectives**
- ✓ to identify vehicles
- ✓ to talk about different types of transportation

**Classroom English**
- Show me. Find. Say. Write. Color. What is it?

**Language Patterns**
- How do you go to (work/school)?
- I go to (work/school) by (bike).

**Materials**
- Crayons and pencils or markers, construction paper, scissors, old magazines, newspapers
- **Picture Cards:** car, bus, subway, airplane, helicopter, bike, taxi, motorcycle

---

## WARMING UP

Show students the transportation Picture Cards for this unit and review them with the class. Model if necessary. Ask students to use a complete sentence when identifying each vehicle. For example: *It's a (motorcycle).*

Place the Picture Cards on the board and ask students: *How do you go to school?* Invite students to respond and to point to the corresponding Picture Card. Model if necessary.

## USING PAGE 96

Help students find page 96 in their books. Read the question at the top of the page and ask students to read with you.

### Version 1

Students can play in groups of two to four or as a class. Show them how to drop the paper clip onto the circle. Each student gets a turn. They must name the item and use it in a

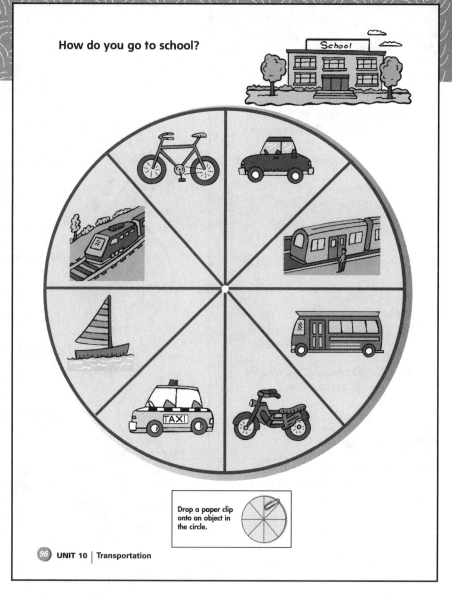

How do you go to school?

Drop a paper clip onto an object in the circle.

question and a response: *How do you go to school? I go to school by car.* Students earn one point for each correct question and response. The student with the most points at the end of the game wins.

### Version 2

This version of the game is an easier version. One student asks the student whose turn it is: *How do you go to school?* The student drops the paper clip and responds with the vehicle the paper clip landed on: *I go to school by (bus).*

## EXTENSION
### Vehicle Books

Show students a vehicle book you have prepared ahead of time. You can either draw pictures, paste in the

Picture Cards, or paste in pictures from magazines or newspapers. Ask students to identify the vehicles. Give each student six pieces of construction paper, and show students how to fold them so that they have twelve pages. Use a hole punch and string and help students assemble their books. Students make a cover and then draw or paste a picture on each page. Students should also label each picture with the vehicle name. Write the vehicle names on the board for students to use as a reference when working. When students are finished, invite them to share their books with the rest of the class. Students can point to each picture and name the vehicle. They can also tell how they go to school: *I go to school by (bike).*

# Units 9 & 10
Review

**Vocabulary:** airplane, bike, boat, bus, car, card, dance, family, fireworks, friend, give, helicopter, make a wish, mask, motorcycle, parade, present, send, subway, taxi, train, visit, watch, wear

## Review Objectives

✓ to identify celebrations

✓ to identify vehicles

✓ to identify adverbs of frequency: *always, never*

✓ to identify feelings: *happy, sad, tired, hungry, thirsty*

## Classroom English

• Listen. Check. Point. Say.

## Language Patterns

• I (never) (give presents) on New Year's Day.

• How do you (go to school)?

• I (go to school) by (train).

## Materials

• **Realia:** mask, card, present

• **Picture Cards:** visit, wear, send, dance, watch, fireworks, parade, mask, make a wish, friend, family, card, give, present, car, bus, subway, airplane, helicopter, bike, taxi, motorcycle

## WARMING UP

Use realia or Picture Cards to review the nouns from Unit 9. Ask: *What is it?* Invite students to use a complete sentence when answering: *(It is/It's) a (present).* Review the celebrations and holidays with students. Show a calendar to remind them when these celebrations take place. Ask students

to tell when their birthdays are and what they do on their birthdays. Ask them to tell how and when they celebrate New Year's Day. Hold up the Picture Cards from Unit 9 to prompt students. Model if necessary.

Use toy vehicles or Picture Cards to review the vehicles from Unit 10. Ask students to name the vehicles. For example: *It's a (taxi).* Encourage

students to use a complete sentence. Model if necessary.

Tape two vehicle Picture Cards to the board and draw a small box under each one. Point to each Picture Card and ask students to tell you which card matches your sentence. Say: *It's a (subway).* Invite a student to place a check in the correct box. Provide additional examples and invite

---

## Review: Units 9 and 10

### Vocabulary
🎧 **A. Listen and check.**

### Always/Never
🎧 **B. Listen and check.**

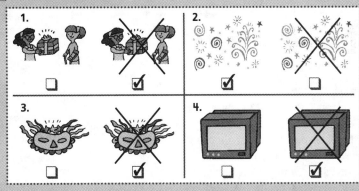

Review | Units 9 and 10 **97**

---

## AUDIOSCRIPT

**A.** 1. helicopter    2. present    3. taxi    4. fireworks    5. mask    6. friends

**B.** 1. I never give presents on New Year's Day.
    3. I never wear a mask on New Year's Day.
    2. I always watch fireworks on New Year's Day.
    4. I never watch TV on New Year's Day.

students to come up and check the correct boxes.

Tape one celebration Picture Card to the board. Write *yes* and *no* under the Picture Card and draw a box next to each word. Say a sentence, such as: *It is a mask.* Students should verify if the sentence you said is correct or incorrect according to the picture. Provide additional examples and invite students to come up and check either the *yes* or *no* box.

If you feel students need to practice exercises that are similar to those presented in the Review Units, use exercises like the one above. You can use similar exercises for any of the Review Exercises at the end of a unit.

## USING PAGE 97

Help students find page 97 in their books. Help students find Exercise A. Read the directions and ask students to follow along. Point to each picture and ask students to say the words with you. Explain to students that they should check the picture that goes with the word that they hear. Play the recording or read the audioscript for students. Students check the correct picture.

Help students find Exercise B. Read the directions and ask students to follow along. Point to the pictures and ask students to repeat each word after you. Explain to students that they should check the box for the picture that matches the sentence they hear. Play the recording or read the audioscript. Students check the correct picture.

## How...?
### C. Listen and check.

## How are you feeling?
### D. Listen, point, and say.

98  Review | Units 9 and 10

## USING PAGE 98

Help students find page 98 in their books. Help students find Exercise C. Read the directions and ask students to follow along. Point to the pictures and ask students to tell how each person goes to school. Explain to students that they should check *yes* if the picture matches the question and answer they hear. They should check *no* if the

picture does not match the sentences they hear. Play the recording or read the audioscript for students. Students check the correct picture.

Help students find Exercise D. Read the directions and ask students to follow along. Explain that they should listen, point to the picture, and then say the question and answer. Play the recording or read the audioscript for students.

## AUDIOSCRIPT

**C.** 1. A: How do you go to school?
   B: I go to school by bike.
4. A: How do you go to school?
   B: I go to school by car.

2. A: How do you go to school?
   B: I go to school by bus.
5. A: How do you go to school?
   B: I go to school by helicopter.

3. A: How do you go to school?
   B: I go to school by train.
6. A: How do you go to school?
   B: I go to school by taxi.

**D.** 1. A: How are you feeling?
   B: I'm sad.

2. A: How are you feeling?
   B: I'm hungry.

3. A: How are you feeling?
   B: I'm thirsty.

4. A: How are you feeling?
   B: I'm happy.

**scissors**

**glue**

**notebook**

**draw**

**open**

**paper**

close

**cut**

squirrel

swing

tree

bench

sun

seesaw

cloud

butterfly

window

computer

telephone

mirror

flower

house

ant

door

bike

pet

radio

sink

supermarket

Mike's Market

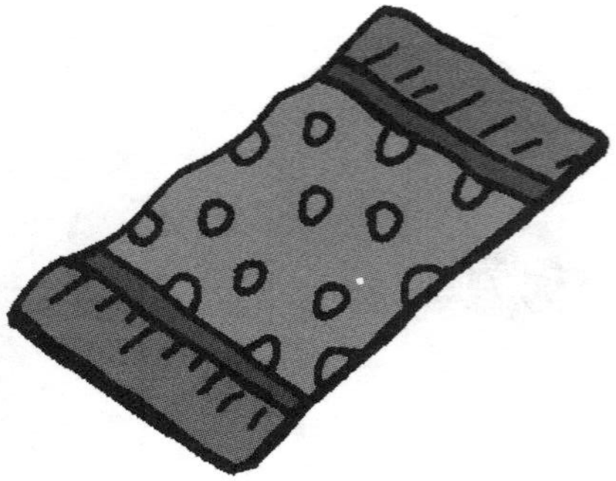

post office

Post Office

bakery

Bakery

rug

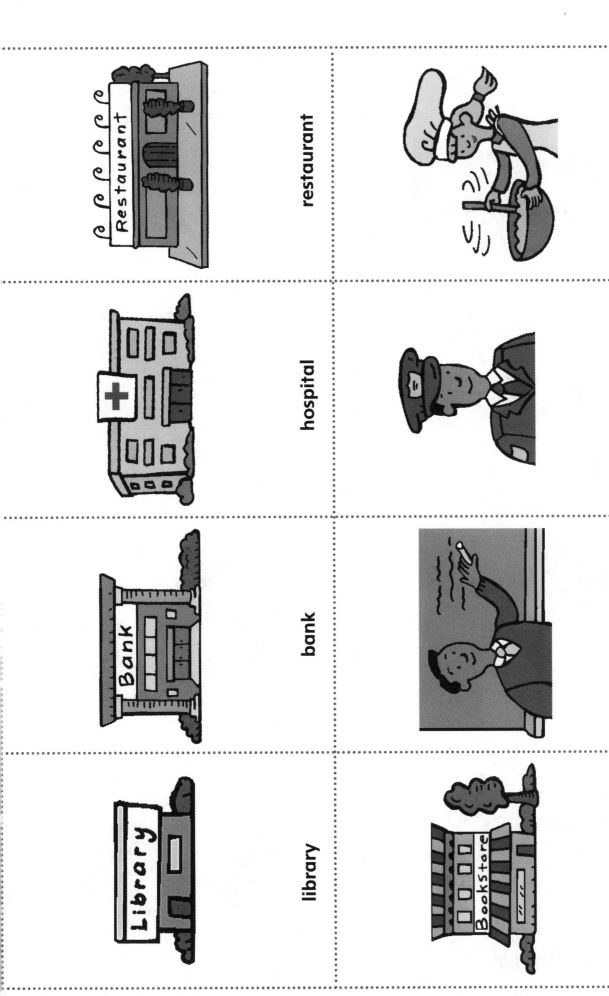

restaurant

cook

hospital

police officer

bank

teacher

library

bookstore

firefighter

mail carrier

doctor

vet

dentist

nurse

clerk

librarian

wake up

play the piano

eat dinner

go home

eat lunch

go to school

eat breakfast

get dressed

water

orange

potato

carrot

go to sleep

tomato

listen to music

onion

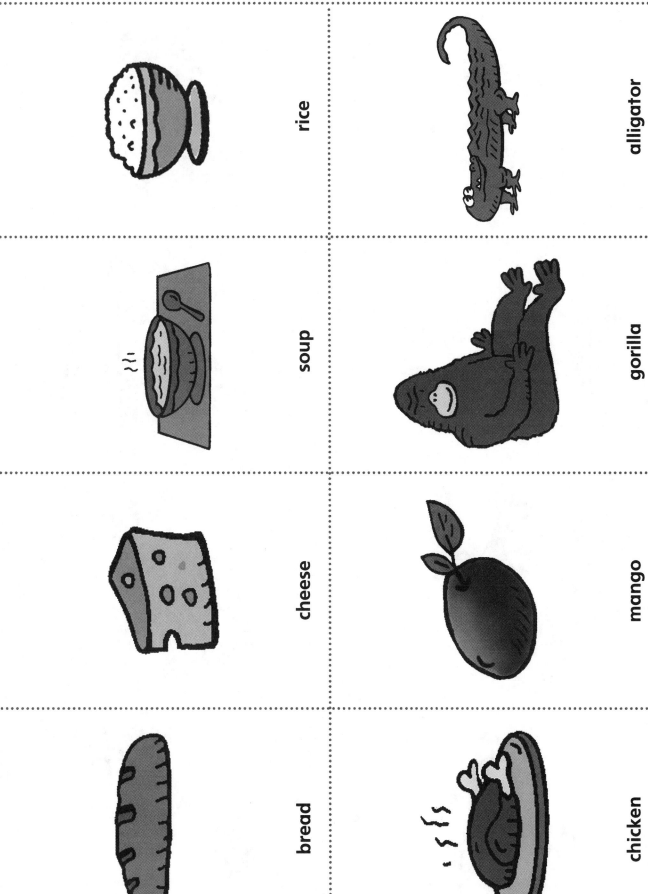

rice

alligator

soup

gorilla

cheese

mango

bread

chicken

tiger

bear

monkey

zebra

seal

panda

lion

giraffe

wear a mask

make a wish

visit family or friends

dance in a parade

elephant

send cards

hippo

give presents

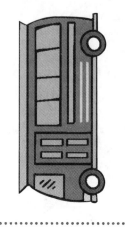

bus

car

helicopter

subway

airplane

motorcycle

watch fireworks

taxi